Table of Contents

Introduction

What Is Close Reading?

Rigorous standards for English Language Arts place new demands on students and teachers. Students are expected to read and comprehend complex literary and informational texts independently and proficiently. One way to achieve this level of text comprehension is through close reading. Close reading features repeated readings of a text with each reading focused on a specific aspect of the text, for instance, vocabulary or text structure. Through the close reading process, students build up their understanding gradually, so by the end they have a thorough understanding of what they read.

What Is Conquer Close Reading?

Conquer Close Reading is a series of reproducible books for Grades 2–6 that helps students learn to engage in a close reading of a text so that over time they can successfully understand, analyze, and evaluate the ideas in complex texts independently. Students first build close reading skills and then practice and apply them so they develop and hone the skills and abilities necessary to comprehend the increasingly complex texts they will encounter.

In Conquer Close Reading, students learn to unlock the meaning of text by:

- Reading and annotating passages in a variety of genres
- Engaging in close readings and collaborative conversations about the texts
- Examining the vocabulary authors use
- Analyzing text structure of both literary and informational texts
- Evaluating the "big ideas" proposed in texts
- Writing about what they've read and discussed using text evidence

Teaching the Building Block Mini-Lessons

Each grade of Conquer Close Reading begins with two sample texts—one literary and one informational—and a series of twelve mini-lessons. The mini-lessons use the passages to build the skills students need to read closely for deep meaning.

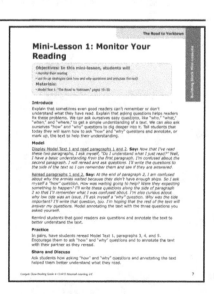

Teaching the Main Passages and Lessons

Each of the fourteen main lessons in Conquer Close Reading features a passage—either literary or informational—that students read and reread to practice and apply the close reading skills they've acquired during instruction of the mini-lessons.

As you start instruction using Conquer Close Reading, keep in mind that students need the opportunity to grapple with the ideas they find in text. They should read the passages independently the first time. Avoid front-loading information or pre-teaching vocabulary. This will allow students to first notice what is confusing so they develop a habit they can use when they read on their own.

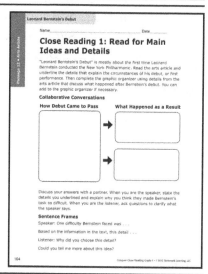

Step 1

The first reading focuses on gaining a general understanding of the text. The students summarize what they read by identifying what the text is mostly about. They also identify key details necessary for understanding. The first reading culminates in a collaborative conversation, giving students an opportunity to build speaking and listening skills, broaden their point of view, and build vocabulary as they compare their impressions of the text and prepare to delve into it in greater detail.

Step 2

The second reading starts the building of a deeper understanding of the text. This reading focuses on four to six vocabulary words: Tier 2 words, challenging words, or examples of figurative language. Students use context to determine word meaning, the connotation in the text, and why the author chose the word.

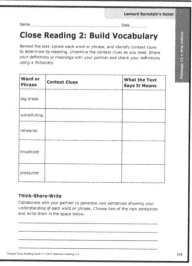

Step 3

The third reading centers on text structure. For informational texts, one of the five basic patterns of text structure is explored, giving students an opportunity to explore the relationship between meaning and text structure. For literary texts, the focus is on how basic story elements interact to bring life to a work of fiction.

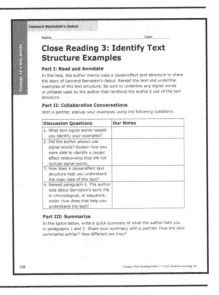

Step 4

The fourth reading focuses directly on the deeper meaning of text. Students make inferences, draw conclusions, and synthesize what a text tells them; consider the broader implications of textual information; and consider the author's purpose and point of view.

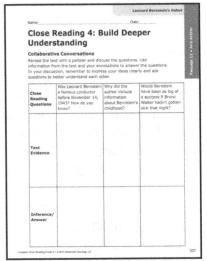

Step 5

Finally, students have an opportunity to write about what they've read. First they analyze a writing prompt based on the text so they know exactly what is expected in their written response. Then they use their annotations, discussion notes, and text evidence as they write a narrative, informative/explanatory, or opinion/argument piece in response to the prompt.

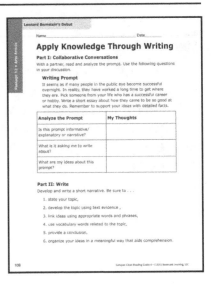

Using the Bonus Tools and Resources

Sentence Resource

The end of each grade-level volume of Conquer Close Reading features resources for students and teachers alike. There is a page of additional sentence frames that students can use during their collaborative conversations.

Writing Checklists

Following the sentence frames are three writing checklists—one each for narrative writing, informative/explanatory writing, and opinion/argument writing. The checklists can be used by students to check their own writing or to conduct peer evaluation. Teachers can also use the checklists to monitor students' progress in developing writing skills.

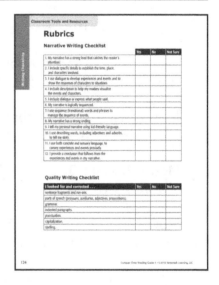

Building Block Mini-Lessons with Model Texts

Mini-Lesson 1: Monitor Your Reading

> **Objectives: In this mini-lesson, students will:**
> • monitor their reading
> • use fix-up strategies (ask *how* and *why* questions and annotate the text)
> **Materials:**
> • Model Text 1: "The Road to Yorktown," pages 19–20

Introduce

Explain that sometimes even good readers can't remember or don't understand what they have read. Explain that asking questions helps readers fix these problems. We can ask ourselves easy questions, like "who," "what," "when," and "where," to get a simple understanding of a text. We can also ask ourselves "how" and "why" questions to dig deeper into it. Tell students that today they will learn how to ask "how" and "why" questions and annotate, or mark up, the text to help their understanding.

Model

Display Model Text 1 and read paragraphs 1 and 2. **Say:** *Now that I've read these two paragraphs, I ask myself, "Do I understand what I just read?" Well, I have a basic understanding from the first paragraph. I'm confused about the second paragraph. I will reread and ask questions. I'll write the questions to the side of the text so I can remember them and see if they are answered.*

Reread paragraphs 1 and 2. **Say:** *At the end of paragraph 2, I am confused about why the armies waited because they didn't have enough ships. So I ask myself a "how" question. How was waiting going to help? Were they expecting something to happen? I'll write these questions along the side of paragraph 2 so that I'll remember what I was confused about. I'm also curious about why low tide was an issue. I'll ask myself a "why" question. Why was the tide important? I'll write that question, too. I'm hoping that the rest of the text will answer my questions.* Model annotating the text with the three questions you asked yourself.

Remind students that good readers ask questions and annotate the text to better understand the text.

Practice

In pairs, have students read Model Text 1, paragraphs 3, 4, and 5. Encourage them to ask "how" and "why" questions and to annotate the text with their partner as they reread.

Share and Discuss

Ask students how asking "how" and "why" questions and annotating the text helped them better understand what they read.

Mini-Lesson 2: Distinguish and Annotate Key Details and Main Ideas

> **Objectives: In this mini-lesson, students will:**
> • distinguish key details from interesting details
> • determine main ideas
> **Materials:**
> • Model Text 1: "The Road to Yorktown," pages 19–20

Introduce

Remind students that texts are made up of key details and main ideas. Texts also include interesting details that are not always important. Tell students that today they will distinguish key details from interesting details so they can determine a main idea. They will annotate the text to help them.

Model

Display Model Text 1 and read paragraph 1. **Say:** *Now that I've read this paragraph, I ask myself, "Which are the key details? Which details are just interesting? What is the main idea of those key details?" Watch me as I analyze and annotate the text to answer my questions.*

Reread paragraph 1. **Say:** *The first sentence sets up the problem, so that is probably a key detail. I'll highlight that sentence. The next sentence is also a key detail, because it connects Washington's troops with French troops. I'll highlight that sentence, too. The third sentence, though interesting, is not really important. I already know the French are fighting with the colonies. The last sentence is also a key detail because it shows that Washington feels he needs the French. I'll highlight that sentence. Now I can see what the key details have in common and determine a main idea.* Model highlighting the text and writing the main idea by the side of paragraph 1. (Main idea: Washington had to join forces with the French to drive the British out of New York.)

Remind students that distinguishing key details from interesting details and annotating them helps determine main ideas.

Practice

In pairs, have students read Model Text 1, paragraph 6. Encourage partners to distinguish key details from interesting details and determine a main idea. Remind them to annotate the text to help them.

Share and Discuss

Invite students to share thoughts and ideas about the text. Ask students to explain how they distinguished key details from interesting details and determined a main idea.

Mini-Lesson 3: Distinguish and Annotate Main Events in a Story

Objectives: In this mini-lesson, students will:
• distinguish main events from details in a story
• annotate main events in a story

Materials:
• Model Text 2: "Sunflowers on the Porch," pages 21–22

Introduce

Remind students that authors base their stories on main events and support those main events with details. Tell students that today they will learn how to distinguish main events from details.

Model

Display Model Text 2 and read paragraphs 1 through 4. **Say:** *These paragraphs have a lot of details in them but only three main ideas. Watch as I distinguish, or separate, the main events from the details.*

Reread paragraphs 1 through 4. As you reread, annotate the text. **Say:** *The first main event is in the first sentence. I know it's a main event because the story is based on this idea. It's about Ambassador Park giving sunflower seeds to students. I'll underline that sentence. The next sentence is a detail. It adds to the story, but it is not an event. The last sentence of this paragraph explains the problem, so it's a main idea. The narrator wants her mom to buy everything needed to plant the seeds. I'll underline that sentence. The information in paragraphs 2 and 3 supports that main idea. These paragraphs are details that make the story flow.*

Repeat the process with the main idea from paragraph 4. **Say:** *Mom wants her child to use items from around the house and to use only one windowsill.* Annotate the main idea to the side of paragraph 4.

Remind students that it is important to distinguish between main ideas and details. Main ideas make up the story. Details add to the story.

Practice

In pairs, have students read paragraph 5. Encourage partners to distinguish between main ideas and details. Ask partners to annotate the text as they work.

Share and Discuss

Invite students to share thoughts and ideas about the text. Ask students to explain how they annotated main ideas.

Mini-Lesson 4: Identify and Annotate Key Words and Phrases

Objectives: In this mini-lesson, students will:
• identify and annotate idioms
Materials:
• Model Text 2: "Sunflowers on the Porch," pages 21–22

Introduce

Remind students that many words in English come from Greek and Latin. The word parts that are still around from those languages are called roots. Explain that learning the roots of words will help students figure out the meaning of new words. Tell students that today they will learn to identify and annotate Latin roots to define unfamiliar words.

Model

Display Model Text 2 and read paragraph 4. **Say:** *In the second sentence of this paragraph, the author uses the word **containers**. Watch as I identify and annotate the Latin roots of this word.*

Reread the second sentence in paragraph 4. After reading, identify and annotate the Latin roots of the word *containers*. **Say:** *The word **container** is made up of two main parts. The first part is **con**. This part comes from the Latin word for "together." You might recognize it from words like **confuse**, **connect**, and **continue**. The second root is **tain**, which comes from the Latin word for "hold." You might have seen it in the words **maintain**, **detain**, and **retain**. So, **contain** means "hold together." A container is something that holds things together in one place.* Annotate the two parts of the word *container*.

Remind students that identifying and annotating Latin roots will help readers better understand the text.

Practice

In pairs, have students read Model Text 2, paragraph 5. Encourage students to annotate the Latin roots of the word *transported*. (*Trans-* means "across," *-port* means "carry.") Encourage them to think of other words they know that have one of these roots (e.g., *transfer, translate, port, airport, porter*).

Share and Discuss

Invite students to share thoughts and ideas about root words. Ask students to explain how they annotated the roots of *transport*, and to share what other words they know with the same roots.

Mini-Lesson 5: Summarize Main Ideas

Objectives: In this mini-lesson, students will:
• combine main ideas into a summary

Materials:
• Model Text 2: "Sunflowers on the Porch," pages 21–22

Introduce

Remind students that summaries are made up of main ideas and very few, if any, details. Readers combine main ideas to help keep summaries very short. Tell students that today they will learn how to combine main ideas to create a summary.

Model

Write these main ideas on chart paper. <u>Read them aloud.</u>

1. Ambassador Park gives students sunflower seeds for Earth Day.

2. The narrator wants her mom to buy pots and dirt for the seeds.

3. Mom wants the narrator to use household items, instead, for planting and to use only one windowsill.

4. The narrator plants seeds and puts them on the windowsill, but she also wants to use the fire escape.

5. She knows the fire escape is off-limits because the landlady said it was only for emergencies.

6. She decides to use the fire escape anyway.

Say: *Now that I've identified the main ideas, I can write a summary by combining main ideas into meaningful sentences.* Model combining the first two main ideas into one sentence: Ambassador Park gives students sunflower seeds for Earth Day, so the narrator wants her mom to buy pots and dirt. **Say:** *I think the third main idea is fine by itself, so I just rewrite it into my summary.* Model rewriting it into the summary.

Practice

In pairs, have students complete the summary using ideas 4 through 6.

Share and Discuss

Ask students to explain how they combined main ideas to finish the summary. To further develop this lesson, model how to reduce the completed summary to three or four sentences.

Mini-Lesson 6: Annotate and Determine Text Structure and Organization

Objectives: In this mini-lesson, students will:

• deconstruct and annotate a text's structure (descriptive)

Materials:

• Model Text 1: "The Road to Yorktown," pages 19–20

Introduce

Explain to students that authors organize their writing in different ways. These are called text structures. It is easier to understand the text if we understand how it is organized. Tell students that today they will learn how to take apart and analyze a text with a descriptive text structure.

Model

Display Model Text 1 and read paragraphs 1–2. **Say:** *I can tell that the author is mostly using a descriptive text structure in these paragraphs. Watch as I model how I can tell.* Reread paragraph 1 and **say:** *At first, it looks as if the author is organizing the text by sequence of events because he includes a date. However, after reading the entire paragraph, I can tell that the author is mostly describing General Washington's situation. I'll write that to the side of paragraph 1.* Write the following to the side of paragraph 1: "Descriptive—Author describes General Washington's situation."

Reread paragraph 2 and **say:** *Paragraph 2 also looks like a sequence of events, at first. However, it actually describes what Rochambeau thought about Washington's plan. He didn't like it. I'll write my ideas about text structure to the side of paragraph 2.* Write the following to the side of paragraph 2: "Descriptive—Author describes Rochambeau's thoughts about Washington's plan."

Remind students that analyzing a text's structure and organization will help them understand the text.

Practice

In pairs, have students read Model Text 1, paragraphs 4 through 6. Encourage students to identify and annotate examples of descriptive text structure for each paragraph.

Share and Discuss

Invite students to share their thoughts and ideas about the text. Ask students to explain how they identified and annotated examples of descriptive text structures.

Mini-Lesson 7: Analyze Opinion/ Argument Prompts

> **Objectives: In this mini-lesson, students will:**
> • read and analyze an opinion/argument prompt
> **Materials:**
> • Mini-Lesson Resources, Opinion/Argument Prompts 1 and 2, page 23

Introduce

Explain to students that a prompt is a way to ask a question. Some prompts ask us to give our opinion. Tell students that today they will learn how to analyze an opinion/argument prompt to better answer the question.

Model

Display and read aloud Opinion/Argument Prompt 1. **Say:** *Now that I've read the prompt for the first time, I need to make sure I understand the vocabulary and content words. For example, the word **depicts** means "shows." So evidence in the text shows that Washington was a risk-taker. Well, what's a risk-taker? **Risk-taker** describes someone who is willing to take risks. Being a risk-taking leader can be a good thing. It can also be a bad thing.*

Next, reread each sentence of the prompt. **Say:** *The first sentence explains the topic. I will be writing about how the text depicts, or shows, General Washington as a risk-taker. The second sentence tells me I need to decide whether I agree or disagree with the statement in the prompt's first sentence. So I give my opinion. The last sentence tells me that I need to use information, or evidence, from the text to support my opinion.*

Remind students that analyzing a prompt will help them write a strong essay that answers the question.

Practice

In pairs, have students read Opinion/Argument Prompt 2. Encourage students to analyze the prompt.

Share and Discuss

Invite students to share their thoughts and ideas about the prompt. Ask students to explain how they analyzed the prompt.

Mini-Lesson 8: Analyze Informative/Explanatory Prompts

Objectives: In this mini-lesson, students will:

• read and analyze an informative/explanatory prompt

Materials:

• Mini-Lesson Resources, Informative/Explanatory Prompts 1 and 2, page 23

Introduce

Explain to students that a prompt is a way to ask a question. Some prompts ask us to provide information or explain something. Tell students that today they will learn how to analyze an informative/explanatory prompt to better answer the question.

Model

Display and read aloud Informative/Explanatory Prompt 1. **Say:** *Now that I've read the prompt for the first time, I need to make sure I understand the vocabulary and content words. For example, the word **outlining** tells me that I'm going identify only the most important ideas and details. I won't need to include the little details.*

Next, reread each sentence of the prompt. **Say:** *The first sentence explains the topic. I will write about the tricks Washington pulled on the British. The tricks happen in paragraphs 6 and 7. So I'll need to pay careful attention to those paragraphs. The second sentence tells me exactly what I'm to write about. I'm asked to outline the tricks. So I'll need to include the big ideas and supporting details for each trick, but I won't need to include the smaller details. The last sentence tells me that I need to use information, or evidence, from the text to support my explanation.*

Remind students that analyzing a prompt will help them write a strong essay that answers the question.

Practice

In pairs, have students read Informative/Explanatory Prompt 2. Encourage students to analyze the prompt.

Share and Discuss

Invite students to share their thoughts and ideas about the prompt. Ask students to explain how they analyzed the prompt.

Mini-Lesson 9: Analyze Narrative Prompts

Objectives: In this mini-lesson, students will:
- read and analyze a narrative prompt

Materials:
- Mini-Lesson Resources, Narrative Prompts 1 and 2, page 23

Introduce

Explain to students that a prompt is another way to ask a question. Prompts ask us to answer different types of questions. Some prompts ask us to write a short story. Tell students that today they will learn how to analyze a narrative prompt to better answer the question.

Model

Display and read aloud Narrative Prompt 1. **Say:** *Now that I've read the prompt for the first time, I need to make sure I understand the vocabulary. For example, the word **narrator** means "the person telling the story." Mrs. Rosa refers to the narrator as "that gardening girl," so I know the narrator is a girl.*

Next, reread each sentence of the prompt. **Say:** *The first two sentences state an observation about the story that is important. The third sentence tells me what I'm supposed to write about. The story doesn't say whether Mrs. Rosa tells the narrator's mother about what happened with the plants. So I'm to write a story about what might have happened had Mrs. Rosa told her mother. The last sentence tells me that I need to use actual events from the story in my narrative.*

Remind students that analyzing a prompt will help them write a strong short story that answers the question.

Practice

In pairs, have students read Narrative Prompt 2. Encourage students to analyze the prompt.

Share and Discuss

Invite students to share their thoughts and ideas about the prompt. Ask students to explain how they analyzed the prompt.

Mini-Lesson 10: Choose Text Evidence That Supports the Prompt

> **Objectives: In this mini-lesson, students will:**
> • identify text evidence that supports the writer's answer to a prompt
>
> **Materials:**
> • Model Text 1: "The Road to Yorktown," pages 19–20
> • Mini-Lesson Resources, Informative/Explanatory Prompt 2, page 23

Introduce

Explain to students that when they are writing to a prompt they must include evidence from the text that supports their answer. Tell students that today they will learn how to identify text evidence that best supports their ideas.

Model

Display and read Informative/Explanatory Prompt 2. **Say:** *I understand what I am supposed to do. This prompt actually gives me a statement that I have to defend. I don't need to come up with my own idea about Rochambeau. Instead, I need to review the text and decide which evidence supports the statement in the prompt.*

Display Model Text 1 and read paragraph 1. **Say:** *After rereading this paragraph, I notice that the first line supports the statement. It says that Washington was desperate for supplies, soldiers, and good news. That means that he knew that American troops could not win alone. He needed Rochambeau and the French. I'll highlight the first sentence and annotate my thoughts. The last sentence in this paragraph also supports the statement. He believed that, together, Americans and French could drive the British out of New York. I'll highlight and annotate that sentence, too.* Model annotating the first paragraph.

Remind students that identifying text evidence that answers the prompt will help them write a strong essay.

Practice

In pairs, have students identify text evidence from paragraphs 2 and 3 that supports the statement in the prompt. Encourage students to consider Washington's relationship with Rochambeau. ("So they waited" suggests that Washington was willing to listen to the thoughts and advice of leaders from other countries.)

Share and Discuss

Invite students to share their thoughts and ideas. Ask students to explain how they identified text evidence to support the answer to the prompt.

Mini-Lesson 11: Collaborative Conversations—Respectfully Responding to Questions

Objectives: In this mini-lesson, students will:
• respond to listeners' questions in a respectful manner
• check for listeners' understanding

Materials:
• Model Text 2: "Sunflowers on the Porch," pages 21–22

Introduce

Remind students that sometimes we must respond to questions about our ideas. Tell students that today they will learn how to respond in a respectful manner and check their listeners' understanding.

Model

Display Model Text 2. Read paragraphs 1 through 4. **Say:** *Listen to my statement about these paragraphs.*

> I think Mom did the right thing by not buying 24 pots. They had plenty of containers. The narrator just needed to use her head a little.

Say: *Let's pretend that you don't understand what I mean. You say, "Tell me more about why you think this way." As the speaker, it is my job to clearly explain my ideas. The listener has every right to ask questions to better understand my point. This two-way dialogue is the basis for a good discussion. When I respond, I remember to speak with a nice tone of voice and use evidence from the text to explain my thoughts. For instance, I could say, "Once she actually bothered to look, the narrator found 24 things to plant in around the house in just a day." Then, to see whether listeners understand, I ask, "Do you understand my idea better now?" to check for understanding.*

Practice

In pairs, have students reread Model Text 2, paragraphs 5 and 6. Encourage students to role-play with the following statement.

> The narrator bent the rules about the fire escape.

Ask one student to be the speaker and one student to be the listener. After the speaker makes the statement, have the listener say, "Tell me more about why you think that way." Encourage the speaker to respond in a respectful manner and check for understanding.

Share and Discuss

Invite students to explain what they learned from this activity.

Mini-Lesson 12: Collaborative Conversations—Listener Clarifies by Restating

> **Objectives: In this mini-lesson, students will:**
>
> • clarify the speaker's words by restating
>
> **Materials:**
>
> • Model Text 2: "Sunflowers on the Porch," pages 21–22

Introduce

Explain that there are many ways to understand, or clarify, what someone has said. Tell students that today they will learn how to clarify what the speaker has said by restating in their own words.

Model

Display Model Text 2. Read the text and **say:** *I'm going to make a statement about this story and then model how to restate what I said using different words.* Read the following statement aloud.

> I think Mrs. Rosa is a very wise woman. She found the narrator on the fire escape talking on the phone and then she found the narrator using the fire escape for her plants. Mrs. Rosa could have caused trouble for the narrator. Instead she found a way to help.

Say: *If I were the listener, I could say something like this.*

> So you are saying that Mrs. Rosa is wise because she thought about why the narrator used the fire escape and figured out a way that might help the situation. Is that right?

Say: *Notice how I didn't repeat what was said word for word. I put the speaker's ideas in my own words and summarized them.*

Remind students to clarify what someone has said by restating it.

Practice

In pairs, have students clarify the following statement in their own words. Ask students to begin with, "So you are saying that . . . "

> I think the narrator will continue to bend the rules. She wasn't punished for using the fire escape again, and Mrs. Rosa didn't tell Mom.

Share and Discuss

Invite students to share their experiences. Ask students to explain what they learned about clarifying by restating in their own words.

Name_____ Date_____

Model Text 1: *The Road to Yorktown*

by Daryl Heller

1   In the summer of 1781, General George Washington was desperate for supplies, soldiers, and good news. For many months, he had gathered his American troops in New Jersey with the hope of joining forces with the French general Rochambeau, whose troops were in Rhode Island. The French had joined the Americans in their war for independence several years earlier. Washington believed that together they could drive the British general Clinton and his forces from New York.

2   Rochambeau would not agree to Washington's plan. The French general knew they were outnumbered by British forces and would need additional ships to damage Clinton's strong defenses. In addition, New York's harbor was shallow, and their attacking ships could easily become grounded at low tide. So they waited.

3   Finally, on August 14, 1781, Washington learned that the French admiral Paul was sailing to the Chesapeake Bay area of Virginia. Paul had a fleet of ships and a great number of soldiers. He had been instructed to help the Americans until mid-October. Now Rochambeau and Washington agreed: They would leave New York and march south to Virginia. They had received news that defeating the British there would be an easier task. But first, they had to get out of New Jersey.

4   Before they could be safely on their way, the French and American forces had to travel past Clinton's troops. The British were stationed just across the Hudson River in nearby Staten Island.

continued

Name_____ Date_____

5   Another danger was that there were many British spies in the area who reported on Washington's every move. If Clinton knew that Washington was marching his men toward Virginia, he would attack. Washington and Rochambeau could not risk losing any men or supplies. They would need them in Virginia.

6   To avoid attack, not only did Washington keep his plans to march to Virginia a secret, but he even tricked Clinton into thinking he was preparing to strike New York. Washington ordered baking ovens built in Chatham, New Jersey. Large ovens would be needed to feed hungry troops. This made it seem as if the Americans would be staying in the area for a while. Since British spies often stole Washington's private letters, Washington made sure to send several messages that described an attack on New York.

7   To further trick the spies, Washington also built a camp at Elizabethtown, New Jersey. The Hudson River was narrow at Elizabethtown. This would make it a good spot for his men to cross the river to battle the British in Staten Island. Washington spread a rumor that he needed to buy boats to take his men across the water, too.

8   Washington and Rochambeau snuck into Trenton, New Jersey, at the beginning of September. The British were still preparing for a battle in New York, but the French and American armies were already speeding to Virginia.

9   Washington's tricks and secrecy paid off. Before the British had a chance to send extra troops to Virginia, Washington's army was already there. The American and French forces surrounded them in Yorktown, Virginia, in October 1781. They captured more than 7,000 British soldiers. The long war in America had been won.

Name_____ Date_____

Model Text 2: *Sunflowers on the Porch*

by Daryl Heller

1   To celebrate Earth Day, Ambassador Park gave students packets of sunflower seeds. Inside were 24 zebra-striped seeds with directions for growing the flowers printed on the back. I called my mom at the office and asked, "Can you please bring home soil and 24 small pots?"

2   "For what?" she asked. I could hear her fingers clattering on a keyboard in the background.

3   "We got sunflower seeds for Earth Day."

4   "I'll purchase one pot and soil. Be resourceful: look around the house for containers we already have, but know that you can place them on only one windowsill. We're not a horticultural center."

5   By the next day, I stood in the kitchen holding an egg carton with twelve pockets for dirt, one new pot, and eleven containers that had once held olives, margarine, or hummus. Once all of these were filled with potting soil and seeds, I transported them to the living room, which was bright most of the day. The windowsill fit six of my twelve containers. For the remainder, I looked longingly beyond the window to the fire escape.

6   I wasn't allowed on the fire escape. Mrs. Rosa, our landlady, caught me talking on the phone out there the first week we moved in. Hanging above the treetops, the fire escape felt like a porch in the suburbs. Mrs. Rosa didn't say anything to me directly. Instead, we received a formal complaint: The fire escape is for emergencies only. The fire escape is not a playground.

continued

Name_____ Date_____

7   But I knew my plants would thrive in the outdoor sun; plus, I wouldn't actually be sitting out there. I set the remaining containers inside a dish tub. Then I lifted the window, looked cautiously below, and laid the tub on the metal grating. I pressed it close to the building, where I hoped it might be overlooked.

8   A week later, the sunflowers on the fire escape had risen to the soil's surface. Some seedlings had pieces of broken shell stuck to their heads like motorcycle helmets; others had sets of tiny green leaves. Unfortunately, this was the same day that Mrs. Rosa finally spotted the tub. This time she left a message on our answering machine: "Get the pots off the fire escape immediately. And tell that gardening girl to come downstairs. I want to have a chat with her."

9   Nervous as I was, I knew I had to see Mrs. Rosa. She threw open the door before I even finished knocking. Donning a pair of eyeglasses, she looked me over, and then pointed to a scraggly rosebush beside the front steps. Around the bush was a large border of dirt. "Once August comes around, that spot looks especially dismal. Why don't you dig a few holes and put your plants there?" I accepted, praying she wouldn't tell Mom about the fire escape.

10   Not all of my seeds took root. Some were eaten by city predators: squirrels and pigeons. The rest jumped up like a team of basketball players, though. By late summer the sunflowers towered over the rosebush. Their large yellow blooms were so heavy that they politely bowed down to me each time I came home. Well, I suppose they bowed courteously to Mrs. Rosa, too.

Mini-Lesson Resources

Opinion/Argument Prompt 1

"The Road to Yorktown" depicts General Washington as a risk-taker. Do you agree or disagree with this statement? Use evidence from the text to support your opinion.

Opinion/Argument Prompt 2

In "Sunflowers on the Porch," Mrs. Rosa gives the narrator space to grow plants. In your opinion, does the narrator deserve this gift? Why or why not? Use evidence from the text to support your opinion.

Informative/Explanatory Prompt 1

In "The Road to Yorktown," the author describes how General Washington tricked British forces. After reading the article, write a short essay outlining each trick. Use evidence from the text in your outline.

Informative/Explanatory Prompt 2

In "The Road to Yorktown," the author suggests that General Washington needed Rochambeau in his quest for victory against the British. After reading the article, write a short essay in which you explain why this is true. Use evidence from the text in your explanation.

Narrative Prompt 1

In "Sunflowers on the Porch," the narrator makes an unlikely friend who keeps a secret. Or does she? After reading the story, write a narrative about what happens when Mrs. Rosa tells the narrator's mom what happened. Use events from the story in your narrative.

Narrative Prompt 2

"The Road to Yorktown" is a nonfiction historical account of the fight for American independence from England. After reading the text, write a short fictional narrative retelling the events from Rochambeau's perspective. Use the first person *I*. Include actual events from the text in your narrative.

Ask Questions Anchor Chart

Questions to Help My Understanding

1. What did you mean when you said _____?
2. Why do you think that way?
3. What evidence from the text makes you think that way?
4. Tell me more about _____.

Table of Contents

Literary Passages

Informational Passages

Name_____ Date_____

Passage 1: Mystery
Our Dad's a Spy!

by Sarah B. Boyle

1   Scott kicked at the crispy brown leaves swirling in windy circles around his feet; it was finally starting to feel like autumn. His twin, Tracy, petted the black cat that wandered around outside their apartment building and cooed, "Hello, Monster."

2   They walked into their apartment, and Tracy picked up a cookbook. "What kind of cake do you think Dad will make for Grandma's birthday?"

3   "Ooh, I hope lemon," Scott replied. "Hey, what's this?" He pulled a crumpled slip of paper from under the dust jacket. It was a list of words and fragments—and the words went in all directions, up and down and backward and forward.

4   "What is Dad doing? Do you think he's a spy?"

5   "And this is his coded message? Awesome!"

6   Just then, Scott and Tracy's dad walked in and said, "I hope you guys haven't been home long; I just went out to grab some eggs to make a cake."

7   Tracy quickly jammed the mysterious piece of paper into her back pocket. Later that night, Scott said, "Let's find out what Dad's up to. Do you have the note?"

8   Then they heard yelling from the kitchen, and their dad poked his head in, looking panicked. "Have you guys seen a paper with a list of words on it?" he asked.

9   "Uh, we haven't seen anything, Dad," Tracy told him. When he left the room, Tracy reached into her back pocket, but the note was gone!

continued

Name_____ Date_____

10   "Do you think Dad's enemies, the guys he is trying to trick, stole it while we were outside after dinner?"

11   "Scott, what if he's involved in something serious?"

12   The following day, Scott and Tracy walked slowly home from school—neither was excited by the idea of facing their dad, who had maybe been lying to them their whole lives about being a spy and not a pastry chef. Suddenly, Scott stopped and leaned into a little nook Tracy didn't remember seeing before.

13   "Is that Monster?" she asked.

14   "Tracy, come closer," Scott said. Nestled safely under the apartment steps, Monster lay on a bed of papers, snuggling a litter of black and white kittens.

15   "Hey, it's Dad's note!" Tracy reached into the nest and pulled it out. "So it wasn't spies that took it."

16   "It was Monster," Scott laughed, and the two headed up the stairs and into their apartment.

17   As Tracy returned their dad's note, Scott asked, "Dad, are you a, um, a spy?"

18   "What? Whatever gave you that idea?" his dad sputtered, shocked.

19   "Well, this note is written in code," Tracy said nervously, with an uneasy giggle.

20   "That's not code; I'm writing a crossword puzzle. Or, I'm trying to," their dad explained.

21   Tracy asked, "So, does that mean you have some cake for us, because you weren't busy being a spy?"

22   Tracy and Scott's dad laughed, and he cut them each a big slice of lemon cake.

Name_____ Date_____

Close Reading 1: Read for Story Elements

"Our Dad's a Spy!" is mostly about a brother and sister who think their dad might be a spy. Read the mystery and underline details that explain the story's plot. Then complete the graphic organizer.

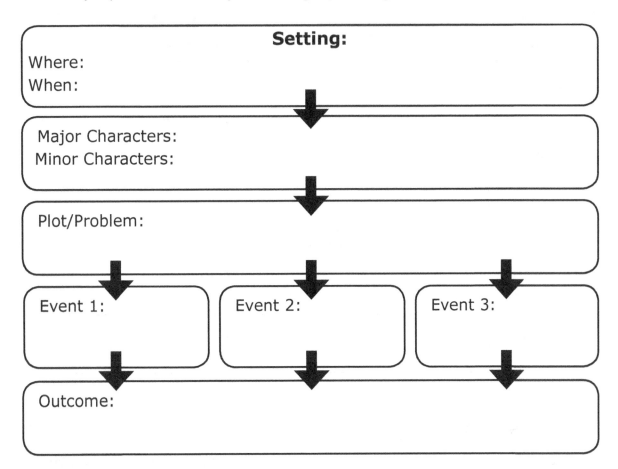

Collaborative Conversations

Discuss your answers with a partner. When you are the speaker, state the details you underlined and explain why you think they are important to the plot. When you are the listener, ask questions to clarify what the speaker says.

Sentence Frames

Speaker: The story focuses on . . .

A key detail that supports the plot is . . .

Listener: Why did you choose this detail?

Could you tell me more about this idea?

Name_____ Date_____

Close Reading 2: Build Vocabulary

Reread the text. Locate each word or phrase, and identify context clues to determine its meaning. Underline the context clues as you read. Share your definitions or meanings with your partner and check your definitions using a dictionary.

Word or Phrase	Context Clues	What the Text Says It Means
swirling		
mysterious		
enemies		
nestled		
nervously		

Think-Share-Write

Collaborate with your partner to generate new sentences showing your understanding of each word or phrase. Choose two of the new sentences and write them in the space below.

_____

_____

_____

_____

_____

Name_____ Date_____

Close Reading 3: Identify Text Structure Examples

Part I: Read and Annotate

In this text, the author mainly uses descriptive text structure to tell the events of the mystery. Reread the text and underline examples of this text structure. Be sure to underline any signal words or phrases used that reinforce the author's use of the descriptive text structure.

Part II: Collaborative Conversations

With a partner, discuss your examples using the following questions.

Discussion Questions	Our Notes
1. What text signal words helped you identify your examples?	
2. Did the author always use signal words? Explain how you were able to identify a relationship that did not include signal words.	
3. How does a descriptive text structure help you understand the main idea of this text?	
4. The author uses descriptive text structure to tell the story, but mysteries also fit the problem/ solution format. Which words in the text help you identify the problems the characters face? Which words help you identify the solutions?	

Part III: Summarize

Write a quick summary of what the author tells you in paragraphs 2–6. Share your summary with a partner. How are your summaries similar? How are they different?

_____

_____

Name_____ Date_____

Close Reading 4: Build Deeper Understanding

Collaborative Conversations

Reread the text with a partner and discuss the questions. Use information from the text and your annotations to answer the questions. In your discussion, remember to express your ideas clearly and ask questions to better understand each other.

Close Reading Questions	Why does the author show Tracy petting Monster in paragraph 1?	How does the mysterious piece of paper end up in Monster's nest?	Why don't the twins just ask their dad if he was a spy?
Text Evidence			
Inference/ Answer			

Name_____ Date_____

Apply Knowledge Through Writing

Part I: Collaborative Conversations

With a partner, read and analyze the prompt. Use the following questions in your discussion.

Writing Prompt

Part of the fun of reading a mystery is that you get to solve the problem right along with the main characters. Write a few paragraphs that describe what you thought the answer to the mystery was. Support your ideas with details from the text.

Analyze the Prompt	My Thoughts
Is this prompt informative/ explanatory or opinion/argument?	
What is it asking me to write about?	
What are my ideas about this prompt?	

Part II: Write

Develop and write a short informative essay. Be sure to . . .

1. state your topic,

2. develop the topic using text evidence,

3. link ideas using appropriate words and phrases,

4. use vocabulary words related to the topic,

5. provide a conclusion,

6. organize your ideas in a meaningful way that aids comprehension.

Name_____ Date_____

Passage 2: Folktale
How Coyote Stole Fire

retold by Sarah B. Boyle

1   There once was a time when people had no fire, and they suffered because of it. They tried to ward off the cold of winter by huddling under blankets, and they ate all their food raw. For Thunder kept fire for himself in a large white rock on top of his mountain, and everyone—even Mountain Lion and Bear—was afraid of Thunder. So fire stayed hidden away from people all over the world.

2   Coyote was a tricky one who wasn't afraid of anything. But more than anything, he loved to make mischief. One day, Coyote decided he would steal fire from Thunder, just for something to do. So Coyote climbed to the top of Thunder's mountain.

3   "Thunder, let's play a game of dice. If I win, you will give me fire. If you win, you can kill me."

4   "Your terms are acceptable. Let's play."

5   Coyote opened a pouch and removed dice made of buffalo teeth. And Thunder gathered a pile of sticks to keep score.

6   Now, Coyote had no intention of losing to Thunder, so he cheated. Whenever Thunder blinked, Coyote flipped the dice so he would win the roll.

7   Near the end of the game, Coyote yelled out, "Oh, Thunder! What a beautiful bird! Look!" When Thunder turned to look, Coyote snatched all his sticks and put them on his own pile. "Why, Thunder, look here. I've won! I have all the sticks!"

8   Thunder rumbled, "How is this possible? I am so confused, but I see you have all the sticks. I suppose you may take fire back down the mountain with you."

Name_____ Date_____

9   Coyote called all the other animals to help him carry away the large white rock that held fire. As the animals gathered around the rock, Thunder realized what had happened.

10   "Coyote, you cheated! Unfortunately, I have no proof. So you can have the fire, but in exchange I will take your life."

11   Coyote knew more tricks than anyone, though, and he could smell trouble before it started. He knew Thunder would figure out he cheated and threaten to kill him. So, when Thunder was distracted by all the other animals, he slipped off his skin—his ears, his fur, his tail, everything—and laid it out near Thunder. Then his insides crept away and hid behind a distant rock.

12   Coyote threw his voice so he sounded like he was right next to Thunder. "I'm right here, Thunder!" he taunted. Thunder was furious and threw the white rock that held fire onto Coyote's skin and fur, breaking it into millions of pieces.

13   The other animals ran to the broken rock and each took a splinter of fire and carried the fire off to tribes all over the world.

14   Meanwhile, Coyote slipped back into his skin. On his way down the mountain, he called over his shoulder to Thunder, "You really shouldn't gamble. You're not very good at it."

Name_____ Date_____

Close Reading 1: Read for Story Elements

"How Coyote Stole Fire" is mostly about how people acquired fire. Read the folktale and underline details that tell you about Coyote's personality. Then complete the graphic organizer using details from the folktale. You can add to the graphic organizer if necessary.

Coyote is . . .	I know because . . .
sneaky	

Collaborative Conversations

Discuss your answers with a partner. When you are the speaker, state the details you underlined and explain why you think they tell the reader about Coyote's character. When you are the listener, ask questions to clarify what the speaker says.

Sentence Frames

Speaker: A key detail about Coyote is that . . .

This detail tells me that Coyote . . .

Listener: Why did you choose this detail?

What evidence in the text leads you to say that?

Name_____ Date_____

Close Reading 2: Build Vocabulary

Reread the text. Locate each word or phrase, and identify context clues to determine its meaning. Underline the context clues as you read. Share your definitions or meanings with your partner and check your definitions using a dictionary.

Word or Phrase	Context Clues	What the Text Says It Means
suffered		
intention		
confused		
realized		
furious		

Think-Share-Write

Collaborate with your partner to generate new sentences showing your understanding of each word or phrase. Choose two of the new sentences and write them in the space below.

_____

_____

_____

_____

Name_____ Date_____

Close Reading 3: Identify Text Structure Examples

Part I: Read and Annotate

In this text, the author mainly uses descriptive text structure to tell the story of how people acquired fire. Reread the text and underline examples of this text structure. Be sure to underline any signal words or phrases used by the author that reinforce the author's use of the descriptive text structure.

Part II: Collaborative Conversations

With a partner, discuss your examples using the following questions.

Discussion Questions	Our Notes
1. What text signal words helped you identify your examples?	
2. Did the author always use signal words? Explain how you were able to identify a relationship that did not include signal words.	
3. How does a descriptive text structure help you understand the main idea of this text?	
4. Reread paragraphs 6 and 7. The author uses sequence words like *now*, *near the end*, and *when*, but the text structure is descriptive. How do these words help you understand the text?	

Part III: Summarize

Write a quick summary of what the author tells you in paragraphs 1 and 2. Share your summary with a partner. How are your summaries similar? How are they different?

_____

_____

Name_____ Date_____

Close Reading 4: Build Deeper Understanding

Collaborative Conversations

Reread the text with a partner and discuss the questions. Use information from the text and your annotations to answer the questions. In your discussion, remember to express your ideas clearly and ask questions to better understand each other.

Close Reading Questions	How do you know this story is a folktale?	Why does Coyote tell Thunder that Thunder can kill him if he loses?	Is Coyote a hero or a villain? Explain your answer.
Text Evidence			
Inference/ Answer			

Name_____ Date_____

Apply Knowledge Through Writing

Part I: Collaborative Conversations

With a partner, read and analyze the prompt. Use the following questions in your discussion.

Writing Prompt

There are many different folktales to explain the same event. Write your own folktale about how people acquired fire. Remember to describe your characters, the setting, and exactly how fire came to be used by people.

Analyze the Prompt	My Thoughts
Is this prompt opinion/argument or narrative?	
What is it asking me to write about?	
What are my ideas about this prompt?	

Part II: Write

Develop and write a short narrative. Be sure to . . .

1. begin the narrative by establishing a situation, including time and place,

2. introduce your characters or the narrator of the story,

3. use dialogue and description to develop characters and events,

4. use signal words to manage the sequence of events,

5. use strong verbs and nouns to explain events and emotions,

6. provide a conclusion,

7. organize the events so that they unfold naturally in the story.

Name_____ Date_____

Passage 3: Poem
Four Tankas

by Sarah B. Boyle

1   A tanka is a five-line poem form that
    originated in Japan. Each line in a tanka has
    a specific number of syllables. The pattern
    is 5-7-5-7-7. In other words, the first line
    has 5 syllables, the second has 7 syllables,
    the third has 5 syllables, and the fourth and
    fifth lines both have 7 syllables. Most tankas
    present one or two simple but beautiful
    images. Then the poet comments on the
    images by relating them to the poet's life. In
    the Japanese tradition, the images are often
    based on elements in the natural world, such
    as animals, plants, and the weather.

2   *Fall*
    a green apple falls
    from the bending fruitful branch
    I bite the crisp flesh
    like the first day back to school
    it tastes cool and sweet and fresh

3   *Winter*
    tight packed white crystals
    glitter in cold weak sunshine
    trapped in a snow globe
    when will the winter relent
    and let us out of the house

continued

Name_____ Date_____

4   *Spring*
    just like a crocus
    pushing its shoots through cold ground
    I shrug off my coat
    and walk through the waking woods
    listen to the songbirds sing

5   *Summer*
    in the green valley
    cool water chuckles and chats
    we shout run and jump
    then listen to our echoes
    shimmering in the noon sun

Name_____ Date_____

Close Reading 1: Read for Poetry Elements

The tankas describe the four seasons in two ways. First, the author describes the season. Second, the author describes how the season affects us. Read each tanka and underline key details that support both parts. Then write the details on the chart.

	Words That Describe the Season	Words That Describe How Humans React to the Season
Fall		
Winter		
Spring		
Summer		

Collaborative Conversations

Discuss your answers with a partner. When you are the speaker, state your ideas and explain how they create an image of each season. When you are the listener, ask questions to clarify what the speaker says.

Sentence Frames

Speaker: This part of the poem makes me think of . . .

The author chose this detail to describe . . .

Listener: Could you tell me more about that detail?

What other details could the author use?

Name_____ Date_____

Close Reading 2: Build Vocabulary

Reread the text. Locate each word or phrase, and identify context clues to determine its meaning. Underline the context clues as you read. Share your definitions or meanings with your partner and check your definitions using a dictionary.

Word or Phrase	Context Clues	What the Text Says It Means
crisp		
relent		
shrug		
shimmering		
trapped in a snow globe		
cool water chuckles		

Think-Share-Write

Collaborate with your partner to generate new sentences showing your understanding of each word or phrase. Choose two of the new sentences and write them in the space below.

_____

_____

_____

_____

Name_____ Date_____

Close Reading 3: Identify Text Structure Examples

Part I: Read and Annotate

In this text, the author mainly uses descriptive text structure to share images of each season with the reader. Reread the text and underline examples of this text structure. Be sure to underline any signal words or phrases used by the author that reinforce the author's use of the descriptive text structure.

Part II: Collaborative Conversations

With a partner, discuss your examples using the following questions.

Discussion Questions	Our Notes
1. What types of figurative language are used in the tankas? Which signal words, if any, helped you identify your examples?	
2. Did the author always use signal words? Explain how you were able to identify figurative language that did not include signal words.	
3. Describe how the author organizes the information presented in each tanka.	
4. The author uses a descriptive text structure while following the syllable count of a traditional tanka. How does the tanka structure affect your understanding of the poems?	

Part III: Summarize

Write a quick summary of what the author wants you to see in "Winter." Share your summary with a partner. How are your summaries similar? How are they different?

_____

_____

Passage 3 • Poem

Name_____ Date_____

Close Reading 4: Build Deeper Understanding

Collaborative Conversations

Reread the text with a partner and discuss the questions. Use information from the text and your annotations to answer the questions. In your discussion, remember to express your ideas clearly and ask questions to better understand each other.

Close Reading Questions	Why does the author choose an apple as the subject for "Fall"?	Compare the sounds of "Spring" and "Summer." How are they alike? How are they different?	What is the mood of "Winter"? Find details that support your answer.
Text Evidence			
Inference/ Answer			

Name_____ Date_____

Apply Knowledge Through Writing

Part I: Collaborative Conversations

With a partner, read and analyze the prompt. Use the following questions in your discussion.

Writing Prompt

A tanka is a five-line poem, usually about animals, plants, and the weather. Write a tanka of your own. Remember to use the syllable pattern 5-7-5-7-7. Describe your subject with rich language to create a vivid image for your reader.

Analyze the Prompt	My Thoughts
Is this prompt informative/explanatory or narrative?	
What is it asking me to write about?	
What are my ideas about this prompt?	

Part II: Write

Develop and write a tanka. Be sure to . . .

1. begin the poem by establishing a situation, including time and place,

2. use a descriptive text structure,

3. use strong verbs and nouns to explain events and emotions,

4. include vivid descriptions to create an image for the reader,

5. follow the 5-7-5-7-7 syllable format.

Name_____ Date_____

Passage 4: Realistic Fiction
Madison's First Day

by Sarah B. Boyle

1   Madison stood at the top of the stairs, looking out over the entire gymnasium. The elite team was practicing advanced moves on the balance beams to her left, and there, on the floor, was a group of girls her age practicing their standing backflips.

2   Madison was excited but tense. Her hands shook a little as she looked down the stairs. Her family had moved to Yellow Springs almost two weeks ago, and the last time she had been in a gymnastics gym was two weeks before that. She had been keeping in shape as best she could at home, but she couldn't wait to feel her body flipping and flying across the mat again.

3   Madison wasn't good at making friends. She was a little shy. It had taken months in her old gym before she made her friends. Now here she was, at the top of the steps to the locker room at the North Star gym. Would any of these girls be her friend? Would it take months of practicing in silence while the other girls chatted and gave one another advice?

4   "Madison! Get down here! Practice started a minute ago," Coach Trish yelled. The girls all looked at Madison, standing there frozen on the steps. And one, the girl wearing the hot pink leotard, started laughing. "Steph, back to work!" Coach snapped.

5   Wasting no more time, Madison darted down the steps and onto the floor mat. She clipped a stray hair back with a barrette and warmed up by doing her splits.

Conquer Close Reading Grade 4 • © Newmark Learning, LLC

Name_____ Date_____

6   "Yikes," Steph said to her. "That's a pretty wimpy split. Can't you get any closer to the floor?"

7   "Madison, our daily warm-up requires five standing backflips," Coach explained. "You can start by standing on a mat or even on a beam if you need a bit of a boost to get all the way around."

8   "Splits like that? No way she can do a standing backflip," Steph sneered to the girl next to her, a quiet girl with glasses and a silver leo. Steph tossed off a backflip like it was no problem at all.

9   *Of course I can do a standing backflip*, Madison thought. All you had to do was jump up and back in the air and then tuck your knees to your chest super fast. It took some courage—and lots of practice.

10   Madison finished her splits and stood up. She flew high, flipping over backward, and landed square with her arms stretched above her head. The girl with the glasses walked over and whispered, "How did you do that? I can't do it without standing at least a foot off the floor."

11   "It's not too hard. I can show you how," Madison offered.

12   "That would be awesome. My name is Lizzy, by the way. And don't mind Steph; she just takes a while to warm up to people."

13   Madison gave a happy sigh and almost cried with relief. The North Star gym was turning out okay.

Name_____ Date_____

Close Reading 1: Read for Story Elements

"Madison's First Day" is mostly about a girl's first day at her new gymnastics gym. Read the realistic fiction and underline the major events in the story. Then complete the graphic organizer using details from the realistic fiction. You can add to the graphic organizer if necessary.

Madison's First Day
First
Next
Next
Next
Next
Last

Collaborative Conversations

Discuss your answers with a partner. When you are the speaker, state the major events you underlined and explain why you think each part was a major event. When you are the listener, ask questions to clarify what the speaker says.

Sentence Frames

Speaker: This event is important because . . .

I know this because . . .

Listener: What details from the story make you think this event is important?

What does this event tell you?

Name_____ Date_____

Close Reading 2: Build Vocabulary

Reread the text. Locate each word or phrase, and identify context clues to determine its meaning. Underline the context clues as you read. Share your definitions or meanings with your partner and check your definitions using a dictionary.

Word or Phrase	Context Clues	What the Text Says It Means
elite		
tense		
silence		
sneered		
backward		
relief		

Think-Share-Write

Collaborate with your partner to generate new sentences showing your understanding of each word or phrase. Choose two of the new sentences and write them in the space below.

_____

_____

_____

_____

_____

_____

Name_____ Date_____

Close Reading 3: Identify Text Structure Examples

Part I: Read and Annotate

In this text, the author mainly uses descriptive text structure to tell about Madison's experiences on her first day at a new gym. Reread the text and underline examples of this text structure. Be sure to underline any signal words or phrases used by the author that reinforce the author's use of the descriptive text structure.

Part II: Collaborative Conversations

With a partner, discuss your examples using the following questions.

Discussion Questions	Our Notes
1. What text signal words helped you identify your examples?	
2. Does the author always use signal words? Explain how you were able to identify a relationship that did not include signal words.	
3. How does a descriptive text structure help you understand the main idea of this text?	
4. Reread paragraph 10. The author tells what happens in sequence even though this text uses a descriptive structure. How does sequence help you understand the text?	

Part III: Summarize

Write a quick summary of what the author tells you in paragraphs 2 and 3. Share your summary with a partner. How are your summaries similar? How are they different?

_____

_____

Name_____ Date_____

Close Reading 4: Build Deeper Understanding

Collaborative Conversations

Reread the text with a partner and discuss the questions. Use information from the text and your annotations to answer the questions. In your discussion, remember to express your ideas clearly and ask questions to better understand each other.

Close Reading Questions	Is Madison more worried about doing well at the gym or making friends there? How do you know?	How does the author feel about Steph? How do you know?	What does the author mean by using the word *square* in paragraph 10?
Text Evidence			
Inference/ Answer			

Name_____ Date_____

Apply Knowledge Through Writing

Part I: Collaborative Conversations

With a partner, read and analyze the prompt. Use the following questions in your discussion.

Writing Prompt

We've all had times when we're the new person in a group. Write about an experience you had as "the new kid." How did you feel when you first joined the group? Describe if those feelings changed, and how.

Analyze the Prompt	My Thoughts
Is this prompt narrative or opinion/argument?	
What is it asking me to write about?	
What are my ideas about this prompt?	

Part II: Write

Develop and write a personal narrative. Be sure to . . .

1. begin the narrative by establishing a situation, including time and place,

2. introduce your characters or the narrator of the story,

3. use dialogue and description to develop characters and events,

4. use signal words to manage the sequence of events,

5. use strong verbs and nouns to explain events and emotions,

6. provide a conclusion,

7. organize the events so that they unfold naturally in the story.

Name_____ Date_____

Passage 5: Fable
The Elephant and the Crocodile

by H. Berkeley Score

1   An Elephant and a Crocodile were once standing beside a river. They were disputing which was the better animal.

2   "Look at my strength," said the Elephant. "I can tear up a tree, roots and all, with my trunk."

3   "Ah! but quantity is not quality, and your skin is not nearly so tough as mine," replied the Crocodile, "for neither spear, arrow, nor sword can pierce it."

4   Just as they were coming to blows, a Lion happened to pass.

5   "Heyday, sirs!" said His Majesty, going up to them, "let me know the cause of your quarrel."

6   "Will you kindly tell us which is the better animal?" cried both at once.

7   "Certainly," said the Lion. "Do you see that soldier's steel helmet on yonder wall?" pointing at the same time across the river.

8   "'Yes!" replied the beasts.

9   "Well, then," continued the Lion, "go and fetch it, and bring it to me, and I shall be able then to decide between you."

continued

Name_____ Date_____

10   Upon hearing this, off they started. The Crocodile, being used to the water, reached the opposite bank of the river first, and was not long in standing beside the wall. Here he waited till the Elephant came up. The latter, seeing at a glance how matters stood, extended his long trunk and reached the helmet quite easily.

11   They then made their way together back across the river. The Elephant, anxious to keep up with the Crocodile in the water, forgot that he was carrying the helmet on his back, and a sudden lurch caused the prize to slip off and sink to the bottom. The Crocodile noticed the accident, so down he dived, and brought it up in his big mouth. They then returned, and the Crocodile laid the helmet at the Lion's feet. His Majesty took up the helmet, and addressing the Elephant, said:

12   "You, on account of your size and trunk, were able to reach the prize on the wall but, having lost it, you were unable to recover it. And you," said the Lion, turning to the Crocodile, "although unable to reach the helmet, were able to dive for it and save it. You are both wise and clever in your respective ways. Neither is better than the other."

13   Moral: Every one has his special use in the world.

Name_____ Date_____

Close Reading 1: Read for Story Elements

"The Elephant and the Crocodile" is mostly about two animals who want to know which of them is better. Read the fable and identify traits of each character. Then complete the graphic organizer using details about each one. You can add to the graphic organizer if necessary.

Collaborative Conversations

Elephant	Crocodile

Discuss your answers with a partner. When you are the speaker, state your ideas and explain why you think each detail is an example of that character's strengths. When you are the listener, ask questions to clarify what the speaker says.

Sentence Frames

Speaker: The author's main point is . . .

A key detail that supports the main idea is . . .

Listener: Why did you choose this detail?

How does that detail help you understand the moral of the story?

Name_____ Date_____

Close Reading 2: Build Vocabulary

Reread the text. Locate each word or phrase, and identify context clues to determine its meaning. Underline the context clues as you read. Share your definitions or meanings with your partner and check your definitions using a dictionary.

Word or Phrase	Context Clues	What the Text Says It Means
disputing		
pierce		
yonder		
lurch		
recover		

Think-Share-Write

Collaborate with your partner to generate new sentences showing your understanding of each word or phrase. Choose two of the new sentences and write them in the space below.

_____

_____

_____

_____

_____

Name_____ Date_____

Close Reading 3: Identify Text Structure Examples

Part I: Read and Annotate

In this text, the author mainly uses descriptive text structure to share the moral of his story. Reread the text and underline examples of this text structure. Be sure to underline any signal words or phrases used by the author that reinforce the author's use of the descriptive text structure.

Part II: Collaborative Conversations

With a partner, discuss your examples using the following questions.

Discussion Questions	Our Notes
1. What text signal words helped you identify your examples?	
2. Does the author always use signal words? Explain how you were able to identify a relationship that did not include signal words.	
3. How does a descriptive text structure help you understand the main idea of this text?	
4. Reread paragraphs 10–12. The author compares the two animals, but the text structure is descriptive. How do these comparisons help you understand the author's message?	

Part III: Summarize

Write a quick summary of what the author tells you in paragraphs 1–9. Share your summary with a partner. How are your summaries similar? How are they different?

_____

_____

_____

Name_____ Date_____

Close Reading 4: Build Deeper Understanding

Collaborative Conversations

Reread the text with a partner and discuss the questions. Use information from the text and your annotations to answer the questions. In your discussion, remember to express your ideas clearly and ask questions to better understand each other.

Close Reading Questions	Why does the Lion ask the Elephant and the Crocodile to bring him the helmet?	Fables often use animals as main characters instead of people. In this story, who does the Lion represent?	Does this story take place in the past, present, or future? How do you know?
Text Evidence			
Inference/ Answer			

Name_____ Date_____

Apply Knowledge Through Writing

Part I: Collaborative Conversations

With a partner, read and analyze the prompt. Use the following questions in your discussion.

Writing Prompt

Fables are written with a particular moral, or lesson, in mind. The moral of this fable is that no one is better than anyone else. But fables can also have more than one moral. Reread the text. What other lesson can be learned from this fable? State your topic and use evidence from the text to support your answer.

Analyze the Prompt	My Thoughts
Is this prompt opinion/argument or narrative?	
What is it asking me to write about?	
What are my ideas about this prompt?	

Part II: Write

Develop and write a short informational essay. Be sure to . . .

1. state your topic,

2. develop the topic using text evidence,

3. link ideas using appropriate words and phrases,

4. use vocabulary words related to the topic,

5. provide a conclusion,

6. organize your ideas in a meaningful way that aids comprehension.

Name_____ Date_____

Passage 6: Poem
My Garden Concert

Anonymous

1   I hear a splendid concert in my garden every day,

   When the breezes find by grove and lawn some instrument to play;

   They shake the shiny laurel with the clatter of the 'bones,'

   And from the lofty sycamore draw deeper cello tones,

   And giving thus the signal that the concert should begin,

   The brook beside the pebbled path strikes up its mandolin.

2   Then all the garden wakes to sound, for not a bird is mute:

   The robin pipes the piccolo; the blackbird plays the flute;

   While high upon a cedar-top a thrush with bubbling throat

   Lifts up to this accompaniment her clear soprano note.

Name_____ Date_____

3   Then by-and-by there softly sounds, beside some flowering tree

The oboe of the dancing gnat, the cornet of the bee.

Such tiny notes—and yet with ease their cadence I can trace,

While overhead some passing rook puts in his noisy bass,

Or from a green and shady copse, a daisied field away,

I hear the jarring discords of a magpie and a jay.

4   The Wind conducts the orchestra, and as he beats the time

The flood of music sinks and swells in melody sublime;

Till, when the darkness deepens and the sun sets in the West,

They all put up their instruments and settle down to rest;

And when I seek my slumber, like the daisy or the bird,

My rest is all the better for the concert I have heard.

Name_____ Date_____

Close Reading 1: Read for Poetry Elements

"My Garden Concert" is mostly about the sounds the author hears in his or her garden. Read the poem and underline the words and phrases in the poem that help you imagine what the author hears. Then complete the graphic organizer using details from the poem. You can add to the graphic organizer if necessary.

My Garden Concert	
Plant/Animal	**Instrument**
sycamore tree	cello

Collaborative Conversations

Discuss your answers with a partner. When you are the speaker, state your ideas and explain the connection between the plant or animal and the sound it makes. When you are the listener, ask questions to clarify what the speaker says.

Sentence Frames

Speaker: The author's main point is . . .

I think the author paired this plant/animal and this instrument because . . .

Listener: Why did you choose this detail?

What evidence in the poem leads you to say that?

Name_____ Date_____

Close Reading 2: Build Vocabulary

Reread the text. Locate each word or phrase, and identify context clues to determine its meaning. Underline the context clues as you read. Share your definitions or meanings with your partner and check your definitions using a dictionary.

Word or Phrase	Context Clues	What the Text Says It Means
strikes up		
mute		
bubbling throat		
discords		
beats the time		
slumber		

Think-Share-Write

Collaborate with your partner to generate new sentences showing your understanding of each word or phrase. Choose two of the new sentences and write them in the space below.

_____

_____

_____

_____

_____

Name_____ Date_____

Close Reading 3: Identify Text Structure Examples

Part I: Read and Annotate

In this text, the author uses elements of poetic text structure, such as rhyme and stanzas, to tell about the sounds of the garden. Reread the text and underline examples of this text structure. Be sure to underline any signal words or phrases used by the author that reinforce the author's use of the poetic text structure.

Part II: Collaborative Conversations

With a partner, discuss your examples using the following questions.

Discussion Questions	Our Notes
1. Which words in stanza 1 signal the use of a rhyme scheme?	
2. Does the author always use the same rhyme scheme? Explain.	
3. How does the author use stanzas to group information in the poem?	
4. Reread the last four lines of the poem. How do these lines act like a conclusion? What images do they present?	

Part III: Summarize

Write a quick summary of what the author tells you in the poem. Share your summary with a partner. How are your summaries similar? How are they different?

_____

_____

_____

Name_____ Date_____

Close Reading 4: Build Deeper Understanding

Collaborative Conversations

Reread the text with a partner and discuss the questions. Use information from the text and your annotations to answer the questions. In your discussion, remember to express your ideas clearly and ask questions to better understand each other.

Close Reading Questions	Does the author really hear a concert in the garden every day? How do you know?	What is a "thrush"? How do you know?	What is the weather like during the garden concert?
Text Evidence			
Inference/ Answer			

Name_____ Date_____

Apply Knowledge Through Writing

Part I: Collaborative Conversations

With a partner, read and analyze the prompt. Use the following questions in your discussion.

Writing Prompt

"My Garden Concert" describes the sounds that fill the author's garden. Even though we may not notice it, we are constantly surrounded by sound. Write a short essay describing the sounds of your favorite place, such as a park, your house, or even an athletic field. Provide vivid descriptions that show both the sounds and personality of your chosen location.

Analyze the Prompt	My Thoughts
Is this prompt opinion/argument or informative/explanatory?	
What is it asking me to write about?	
What are my ideas about this prompt?	

Part II: Write

Develop and write a short informative essay. Be sure to . . .

1. state your topic,

2. develop the topic using text evidence,

3. link ideas using appropriate words and phrases,

4. use vocabulary words related to the topic,

5. provide a conclusion,

6. organize your ideas in a meaningful way that aids comprehension.

Name_____ Date_____

Passage 7: Historical Fiction
excerpt from *A Connecticut Yankee in King Arthur's Court*

by Mark Twain

1   *Hank Morgan, of Hartford, Connecticut, is the foreman of a weapons factory. In a fight with a worker, he is hit in the head with a crowbar. When Hank awakens, he is sitting under a tree—but he is now in England during the time of King Arthur and the Knights of the Round Table. In this excerpt from the novel, Hank comes across a page, or a young helper to a knight, and describes their conversation.*

2   He began to talk and laugh, in happy, thoughtless, boyish fashion, as we walked along, and made himself old friends with me at once. He asked me all sorts of questions about myself and about my clothes, but never waited for an answer—always chattered straight ahead, as if he didn't know he had asked a question and wasn't expecting any reply, until at last he happened to mention that he was born in the beginning of the year 513.

3   It made the cold chills creep over me! I stopped and said, a little faintly, "Maybe I didn't hear you just right. Say it again—and say it slow. What year was it?"

4   "513."

5   "513! You don't look it! Come, my boy, I am a stranger and friendless. Be honest and honorable with me. Are you in your right mind?"

6   He said he was.

7   "Are these other people in their right minds?"

continued →

Name_____ Date_____

8   He said they were.

9   "And this isn't an asylum? I mean, it isn't a place where they cure crazy people?"

10   He said it wasn't.

11   "Well, then," I said, "either I am a lunatic, or something just as awful has happened. Now tell me, honest and true, where am I?"

12   "IN KING ARTHUR'S COURT."

13   I waited a minute, to let that idea shudder its way home, and then said, "And according to your notions, what year is it now?"

14   "528—nineteenth of June."

15   I felt a mournful sinking at the heart, and muttered, "I shall never see my friends again— never, never again. They will not be born for more than thirteen hundred years yet."

16   I seemed to believe the boy, I didn't know why. Something in me seemed to believe him—my consciousness, as you may say, but my reason didn't. My reason straightway began to clamor. That was natural. I didn't know how to go about satisfying it, because I knew that the testimony of men wouldn't serve—my reason would say they were lunatics, and throw out their evidence. But all of a sudden I stumbled on the very thing, just by luck. I knew that the only total eclipse of the sun in the first half of the sixth century occurred on the 21st of June, A.D. 528, and began at 3 minutes after 12 noon. I also knew that no total eclipse of the sun was due in what to me was the present year—i.e., 1879. So, if I could keep my anxiety and curiosity from eating the heart out of me for forty eight hours, I should then find out for certain whether this boy was telling me the truth or not.

Name_____ Date_____

Close Reading 1: Read for Story Elements

"A Connecticut Yankee in King Arthur's Court" is mostly about a man who has been transported back to the year 528. Read the historical fiction and underline words and phrases that describe the problem faced by the main character. Then complete the graphic organizer using details from the historical fiction. You can add to the graphic organizer if necessary.

A Connecticut Yankee in King Arthur's Court

Setting: **Time:**   **Place:**

↓

Characters:

↓

Problem:

Collaborative Conversations

Discuss your answers with a partner. When you are the speaker, state details you underlined and explain why you think they best describe the main character's problem. When you are the listener, ask questions to clarify what the speaker says.

Sentence Frames

Speaker: The biggest problem the main character faces is . . .

What details does the author provide to describe the problem?

Listener: What evidence in the text leads you to say that?

Could you tell me more about this idea?

Name_____ Date_____

Close Reading 2: Build Vocabulary

Reread the text. Locate each word or phrase, and identify context clues to determine its meaning. Underline the context clues as you read. Share your definitions or meanings with your partner and check your definitions using a dictionary.

Word or Phrase	Context Clues	What the Text Says It Means
honorable		
in your right mind		
asylum		
mournful		
occurred		

Think-Share-Write

Collaborate with your partner to generate new sentences showing your understanding of each word or phrase. Choose two of the new sentences and write them in the space below.

_____

_____

_____

_____

_____

_____

_____

Name_____ Date_____

Close Reading 3: Identify Text Structure Examples

Part I: Read and Annotate

In this text, the author mainly uses descriptive text structure to introduce the problem faced by the main character. Reread the text and underline examples of this text structure. Be sure to underline any signal words or phrases used by the author that reinforce the author's use of the descriptive text structure.

Part II: Collaborative Conversations

With a partner, discuss your examples using the following questions.

Discussion Questions	Our Notes
1. What text signal words helped you identify your examples?	
2. Did the author always use signal words? Explain how you were able to identify a relationship that did not include signal words.	
3. How does a descriptive text structure help you understand the main idea of this text?	
4. Even though the author uses descriptive text structure to tell his story, he also uses sequence signal words like *began* and *at last*. How do these words help you understand the text?	

Part III: Summarize

Write a quick summary of what the author tells you in paragraph 15. Share your summary with a partner. How are your summaries similar? How are they different?

_____

_____

Name_____ Date_____

Close Reading 4: Build Deeper Understanding

Collaborative Conversations

Reread the text with a partner and discuss the questions. Use information from the text and your annotations to answer the questions. In your discussion, remember to express your ideas clearly and ask questions to better understand each other.

Close Reading Questions	How does Hank feel when he realizes that he has traveled back in time?	How old is the page? How do you know?	What does Hank mean by "You don't look it!" in paragraph 5?
Text Evidence			
Inference/ Answer			

Conquer Close Reading Grade 4 • © Newmark Learning, LLC

Name_____ Date_____

Apply Knowledge Through Writing

Part I: Collaborative Conversations

With a partner, read and analyze the prompt. Use the following questions in your discussion.

Writing Prompt

This isn't a story about space or astronomy, so why did the author include so much information about the solar eclipse at the end of the passage? Write a few paragraphs explaining why, being sure to cite text evidence in your answer.

Analyze the Prompt	My Thoughts
Is this prompt informative/ explanatory or opinion/argument?	
What is it asking me to write about?	
What are my ideas about this prompt?	

Part II: Write

Develop and write a short informative essay. Be sure to . . .

1. state your topic,

2. develop the topic using text evidence,

3. link ideas using appropriate words and phrases,

4. use vocabulary words related to the topic,

5. provide a conclusion,

6. organize your ideas in a meaningful way that aids comprehension.

Name_____ Date_____

Passage 8: Social Studies Article
Connecting the Continent
by Sarah B. Boyle

1   In the 1800s, railroads and steam engines crisscrossed the eastern United States. But not a single one crossed the country from east to west. The American West was a land of opportunity and promise. Many were making the difficult journey across the country in order to start new lives. But they journeyed in covered wagons, on horses, or on foot. The journey was long, expensive, and difficult. People, and their horses, often died along the way.

2   Starting in 1863, two companies set out to change the way people traveled across the country. Together they laid more than 2,000 miles of track and built the first Transcontinental Railroad. (*Transcontinental* means "across a continent.") The Union Pacific Railroad Company began building in Council Bluffs, Iowa, where the country's existing railway lines ended. They built westward. The Central Pacific Railroad Company began in Sacramento, California, and built eastward.

3   Building the Transcontinental Railroad was difficult, to say the least. The Central Pacific Railroad laid track across and through the Sierra Nevada Mountains. Their workers used nitroglycerin, a dangerous explosive, to hollow out mountain tunnels. Other workers hung suspended along steep cliffs, hand carving ledges wide and flat enough to support train tracks.

4   The workers of the Union Pacific Railroad graded, or evened out, the land of the Great Plains, which is more rolling than perfectly flat. They spread dirt and gravel across the ground to make the railway lines perfectly flat. Only then could they lay the tracks. Then they moved a little farther west and started the process again.

Name_____ Date_____

5   Despite these challenges, the project was a success. On May 10, 1869, the tracks of the two railroad companies met in Promontory, Utah. A great festival was held to celebrate the achievement. After many speeches, a railroad official drove the final spike of the Transcontinental Railroad, officially connecting the two separate tracks. The journey across the continent once took months and thousands of dollars. Now it took only five days and $150.

6   And the country would never be the same. Towns popped up along the railroad tracks, growing at the same pace as the railroad. Chinese immigrants arrived in California to build the railroad for the Central Pacific Railroad and stayed after they finished their work.

7   Most important, though, the country was united in a way it never had been before. Before, people had lived their lives in their towns, rarely going any farther than they could walk or ride a horse. Now people could easily go anywhere in the country. The country's economy expanded rapidly. Goods traveled along the rails to the towns growing throughout the West.

8   Also, communication was quick and easy. People could move thousands of miles from their families and still remain part of their lives. No other country had so many people who could stay in such close contact.

9   The Transcontinental Railroad changed the way Americans lived and communicated. And it helped turn the United States into the economic superpower it is today.

Name_____ Date_____

Close Reading 1: Read for Main Ideas and Details

"Connecting the Continent" is mostly about the railroad built to connect the eastern and western United States. Read the social studies article and underline the details that support the main idea. Then complete the graphic organizer using details from the social studies article. You can add to the graphic organizer if necessary.

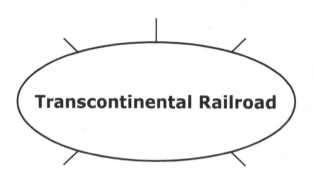

Transcontinental Railroad

Collaborative Conversations

Discuss your answers with a partner. When you are the speaker, state the details you identified and explain why you think they support the main idea of the article. When you are the listener, ask questions to clarify what the speaker says.

Sentence Frames

Speaker: The main idea of this article is . . .

A key detail that supports the main idea is . . .

Listener: Why did you choose this detail?

Could you tell me more about this idea?

Name_____ Date_____

Close Reading 2: Build Vocabulary

Reread the text. Locate each word or phrase, and identify context clues to determine its meaning. Underline the context clues as you read. Share your definitions or meanings with your partner and check your definitions using a dictionary.

Word or Phrase	Context Clues	What the Text Says It Means
expensive		
transcontinental		
existing		
challenges		
celebrate		

Think-Share-Write

Collaborate with your partner to generate new sentences showing your understanding of each word or phrase. Choose two of the new sentences and write them in the space below.

_____

_____

_____

Name_____ Date_____

Close Reading 3: Identify Text Structure Examples

Part I: Read and Annotate

In this text, the author mainly uses descriptive text structure to tell the story of the Transcontinental Railroad. Reread the text and underline examples of this text structure. Be sure to underline any signal words or phrases used by the author that reinforce the author's use of the descriptive text structure.

Part II: Collaborative Conversations

With a partner, discuss your examples using the following questions.

Discussion Questions	Our Notes
1. What text signal words helped you identify your examples?	
2. Did the author always use signal words? Explain how you were able to identify a relationship that did not include signal words.	
3. How does a descriptive text structure help you understand the main idea of this text?	
4. Reread paragraphs 5 and 7. The author uses compare/contrast words like *once* and *now*, but the text structure is descriptive. How do these words help you understand the text?	

Part III: Summarize

Write a quick summary of what the author tells you in paragraphs 3 and 4. Share your summary with a partner. How are your summaries similar? How are they different?

_____

_____

_____

Name_____ Date_____

Close Reading 4: Build Deeper Understanding

Collaborative Conversations

Reread the text with a partner and discuss the questions. Use information from the text and your annotations to answer the questions. In your discussion, remember to express your ideas clearly and ask questions to better understand each other.

Close Reading Questions	Why weren't there any cross-country railroads in the United States prior to 1863?	How did the Transcontinental Railroad contribute to the growth of the United States?	Did the Transcontinental Railroad make the United States seem larger or smaller? Why?
Text Evidence			
Inference/ Answer			

Name_____ Date_____

Apply Knowledge Through Writing

Part I: Collaborative Conversations

With a partner, read and analyze the prompt. Use the following questions in your discussion.

Writing Prompt

What do you think was the most important contribution of the Transcontinental Railroad? Write a brief essay explaining the greatest benefit of the railroad. Be sure to support your opinion with evidence from the text.

Analyze the Prompt	My Thoughts
Is this prompt narrative or opinion/argument?	
What is it asking me to write about?	
What are my ideas about this prompt?	

Part II: Write

Develop and write a short opinion essay. Be sure to . . .

1. introduce the topic,

2. state your opinion,

3. support your opinion with reasons based on text evidence,

4. use linking words and phrases that connect your opinion and reasons,

5. provide a conclusion,

6. organize your ideas in a meaningful way to support your opinion.

Name_____ Date_____

Passage 9: Science Article
Chemistry in the Kitchen

by Sarah B. Boyle

1   You sit down at a fancy restaurant and order a glass of apple juice. You get a pile of jiggling, translucent spheres piled on a glass saucer. You wonder to yourself, *What is this?* And then you pop a sphere into your mouth. The skin of the sphere gives way to the bright clean flavor of apple juice. Amazing!

2   Chefs all around the world are using science to turn everyday flavors into high-tech cuisine—just like those jiggling apple juice spheres. It's called molecular gastronomy.

3   Let's take a closer look at that term *molecular gastronomy*. Gastronomy is the art of cooking. That's what all chefs do. But when you add science to gastronomy—like the chefs who came up with those apple spheres—you get molecular gastronomy. *Molecular* is a science word that means "relating to molecules." Molecules are the tiny building blocks that are visible only with a microscope. So, then, what is molecular gastronomy? It's the art and science of bringing molecules together or splitting them apart in order to make delicious food.

continued

Passage 9 • Science Article

Name_____ Date_____

4   So, how does a chef turn apple juice into a cluster of wiggling spheres that melt in your mouth? She uses a process called spherification. Spherification is just what it sounds like: turning something into spheres. First, the chef prepares a water bath, which is water with special chemicals dissolved in it. Then, she loads the apple juice into a syringe (similar to the kind doctors use when they give shots). Finally, she squeezes the juice out of the syringe, drop by drop, into the water bath. As each drop hits the water, the special chemicals in the bath turn it into a perfect sphere.

5   But don't think molecular gastronomy is all fancy and complicated. Chefs also use science to make simple dishes extraordinary. Take your basic steak. A popular technique for cooking steak is called sous vide (pronounced SOO VEED). *Sous vide* means "under vacuum." When a chef cooks a steak using the sous vide method, he vacuum-seals the steak in a plastic bag. That is, he uses a machine that sucks all the air out of the bag so it clings tightly to the steak. Then he puts that steak into a container of hot water. Special equipment keeps the water at the exact same temperature for long periods of time. After 45 minutes in hot water, the steak is perfectly tender and juicy.

6   The chefs who practice molecular gastronomy spend hours, weeks, sometimes months perfecting a recipe. They often invent techniques and repurpose tools just to create one scrumptious dish. And people pay through the nose to eat those dishes. But don't think you need to be rich and famous to taste this food. You can make it yourself at home. All it takes to make spheres of your own is a kit from the Internet and the desire to experiment.

Name_____ Date_____

Close Reading 1: Read for Main Ideas and Details

"Chemistry in the Kitchen" is mostly about a type of cooking called molecular gastronomy. Read the science article and underline the details that help you understand the subject of the text. Then complete the graphic organizer using details you underlined from the science article. You can add to the graphic organizer if necessary.

Molecular Gastronomy

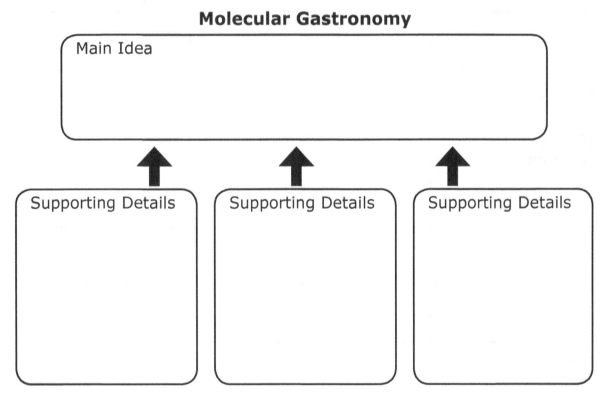

Collaborative Conversations

Discuss your answers with a partner. When you are the speaker, state the details you underlined from the article and explain why you think these details help you better understand the subject of the text. When you are the listener, ask questions to clarify what the speaker says.

Sentence Frames

Speaker: A key detail that helps me understand the subject of the text is . . .

This detail helps me because . . .

Listener: Why did you choose this detail?

What does this detail tell you?

Name_____ Date_____

Close Reading 2: Build Vocabulary

Reread the text. Locate each word or phrase, and identify context clues to determine its meaning. Underline the context clues as you read. Share your definitions or meanings with your partner and check your definitions using a dictionary.

Word or Phrase	Context Clues	What the Text Says It Means
flavor		
molecular gastronomy		
temperature		
techniques		
experiment		

Think-Share-Write

Collaborate with your partner to generate new sentences showing your understanding of each word or phrase. Choose two of the new sentences and write them in the space below.

_____

_____

_____

Name_____ Date_____

Close Reading 3: Identify Text Structure Examples

Part I: Read and Annotate

In this text, the author mainly uses descriptive text structure to explain the subject of the text. Reread the text and underline examples of this text structure. Be sure to underline any signal words or phrases used by the author that reinforce the author's use of the descriptive text structure.

Part II: Collaborative Conversations

With a partner, discuss your examples using the following questions.

Discussion Questions	Our Notes
1. What text signal words helped you identify your examples?	
2. Does the author always use signal words? Explain how you were able to identify a relationship that did not include signal words.	
3. How does a descriptive text structure help you understand the subject of this text?	
4. Reread paragraph 4. The author uses sequence words like *first*, *then*, and *finally*, but the text structure is descriptive. How do these words help you understand the text?	

Part III: Summarize

Write a quick summary of what the author tells you in paragraphs 3 and 6. Share your summary with a partner. How are your summaries similar? How are they different?

_____

_____

_____

_____

Name_____ Date_____

Close Reading 4: Build Deeper Understanding

Collaborative Conversations

Reread the text with a partner and discuss the questions. Use information from the text and your annotations to answer the questions. In your discussion, remember to express your ideas clearly and ask questions to better understand each other.

Close Reading Questions	Why would someone want to go to a restaurant that uses molecular gastronomy?	Is molecular gastronomy hard to do? Why or why not?	How can science change the food we eat?
Text Evidence			
Inference/ Answer			

Name_____ Date_____

Apply Knowledge Through Writing

Part I: Collaborative Conversations

With a partner, read and analyze the prompt. Use the following questions in your discussion.

Writing Prompt

Is molecular gastronomy the best way to prepare food, is it just a waste of time, or something in between? Write a short essay that shares your thoughts about the blending of science and cooking. Would you want to eat this type of food regularly? Why or why not? Use a descriptive text structure to explain your view of molecular gastronomy.

Analyze the Prompt	My Thoughts
Is this prompt informative/ explanatory or opinion/argument?	
What is it asking me to write about?	
What are my ideas about this prompt?	

Part II: Write

Develop and write a short opinion essay. Be sure to . . .

1. introduce the topic,

2. state your opinion,

3. support your opinion with reasons based on text evidence,

4. use linking words and phrases that connect your opinion and reasons,

5. provide a conclusion,

6. organize your ideas in a meaningful way to support your opinion.

Name_____ Date_____

Passage 10: Social Studies Article
Lewis and Clark Meet the Shoshone
from America's Library

1   Meriwether Lewis and William Clark are best known for their expedition from the Mississippi River to the West Coast and back. The expedition, called the Corps of Discovery, was President Thomas Jefferson's visionary project to explore the American West. It began in May of 1804 and ended in September 1806.

2   In August 1805, Lewis and Clark were looking for the Shoshone Indians. The Corps (Lewis and Clark's expedition party) needed horses to cross the Rockies, and the Shoshone had them. Sacajawea, a member of the Corps, was Shoshone, but she had been kidnapped by another tribe many years before.

3   The Corps were still recovering from their portage (the carrying of boats and goods over land) around the Great Falls of Missouri. Morale was low. Lewis and three men were scouting ahead when they finally met a band of Shoshone. They were the first white men the Shoshone had ever seen.

4   Lewis wanted the Shoshone to know that he and his men came in peace. He gave them gifts and used sign language, a few Shoshone words, and red paint (the Shoshone color for peace) to tell them. Luckily, the Shoshone band and their chief, Cameahwait, were convinced.

Name_____ Date_____

5   They celebrated the peaceful meeting with hugs, shouts, and smoking a peace pipe. Lewis wrote many pages about this day in his journal and included a drawing of the peace pipe. Lewis explained that the Shoshone took off their shoes to say they would "always go barefoot if they are not sincere; a pretty heavy penalty if they are to march throughout the plains of their country."

6   Although the Shoshone welcomed Lewis, they were suspicious. They had recently been raided by another tribe. When Lewis asked them to travel to meet the rest of his expedition party, the Shoshone worried that Lewis might be leading them into a trap. Eventually, Lewis convinced them. But when they got to the meeting place, Clark and the others had not yet arrived. So they waited.

7   The Shoshone were nervous about the unknown dangers of the meeting. They didn't want to be ambushed. Lewis was nervous. He had to get horses or the Corps wouldn't be able to finish the expedition. If Clark and the others didn't show up soon, the Shoshone would leave and take their horses with them.

8   Finally, on August 17, 1805, the rest of the Corps arrived. Sacajawea and another member of the Corps were the first to see Lewis and the Shoshone. Sacajawea recognized the area as her home, and now she recognized this band of Shoshone as her people. In fact, Chief Cameahwait was her brother! Everyone celebrated this lucky coincidence. They even named the meeting place Camp Fortunate. Now Lewis and Clark could continue their expedition with Shoshone horses.

Name_____ Date_____

Close Reading 1: Read for Main Ideas and Details

"Lewis and Clark Meet the Shoshone" is mostly about Meriwether Lewis's meeting with the Shoshone Indians. Read the social studies article and underline the details that tell how the meeting occurred and what happened. Then complete the graphic organizer using details from the social studies article. You can add to the graphic organizer if necessary.

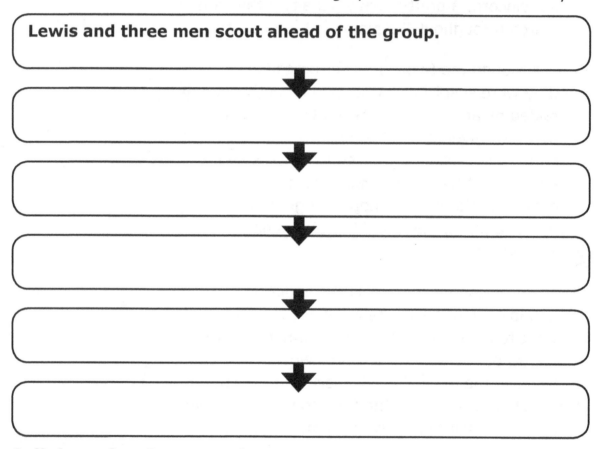

Lewis and three men scout ahead of the group.

Collaborative Conversations

Discuss your answers with a partner. When you are the speaker, state your ideas and explain why the author included that information in the text. When you are the listener, ask questions to clarify what the speaker says.

Sentence Frames

Speaker: A key detail that supports the main idea is . . .

I think this detail is important for understanding the text because . . .

Listener: Why did you choose this detail?

Why did the author include this detail in the text?

Name_____ Date_____

Close Reading 2: Build Vocabulary

Reread the text. Locate each word or phrase, and identify context clues to determine its meaning. Underline the context clues as you read. Share your definitions or meanings with your partner and check your definitions using a dictionary.

Word or Phrase	Context Clues	What the Text Says It Means
expedition		
Corps		
convinced		
journal		
suspicious		
ambushed		

Think-Share-Write

Collaborate with your partner to generate new sentences showing your understanding of each word or phrase. Choose two of the new sentences and write them in the space below.

_____

_____

_____

_____

Name_____ Date_____

Close Reading 3: Identify Text Structure Examples

Part I: Read and Annotate

In this text, the author mainly uses sequence text structure to tell about the meeting between Meriwether Lewis and the Shoshone. Reread the text and underline examples of this text structure. Be sure to underline any signal words or phrases used by the author that reinforce the author's use of the sequence text structure.

Part II: Collaborative Conversations

With a partner, discuss your examples using the following questions.

Discussion Questions	Our Notes
1. What text signal words helped you identify your examples?	
2. Does the author always use signal words? Explain how you were able to identify a sequence relationship that did not include signal words.	
3. How does a sequence text structure help you understand the main idea of this text?	
4. Reread the second and last paragraphs of the text. The author states a problem in the second paragraph and ends the text with the solution even though the text structure is sequence. How does this additional structure help you understand the text?	

Part III: Summarize

Write a quick summary of what the author tells you in paragraphs 4 and 5. Share your summary with a partner. How are your summaries similar? How are they different?

_____

_____

Name_____ Date_____

Close Reading 4: Build Deeper Understanding

Collaborative Conversations

Reread the text with a partner and discuss the questions. Use information from the text and your annotations to answer the questions. In your discussion, remember to express your ideas clearly and ask questions to better understand each other.

Close Reading Questions	Why was the meeting with the Shoshone so important?	Why was it a good thing that Sacajawea was a member of the Corps?	Why did Lewis use gifts and sign language to tell the Shoshone that he and his men came in peace?
Text Evidence			
Inference/ Answer			

Name_____ Date_____

Apply Knowledge Through Writing

Part I: Collaborative Conversations

With a partner, read and analyze the prompt. Use the following questions in your discussion.

Writing Prompt

The Shoshone put a lot of trust in Meriwether Lewis as they waited for the rest of his group to arrive. Imagine that you are one of the Shoshone waiting with Lewis. Write a short story describing your feelings, worries, and fears. Make sure to explain why your tribe decided to wait for the rest of the Corps instead of heading for safety.

Analyze the Prompt	My Thoughts
Is this prompt narrative or informative/explanatory?	
What is it asking me to write about?	
What are my ideas about this prompt?	

Part II: Write

Develop and write a short story. Be sure to . . .

1. begin the narrative by establishing a situation, including time and place,

2. introduce your characters or the narrator of the story,

3. use dialogue and description to develop characters and events,

4. use signal words to manage the sequence of events,

5. use strong verbs and nouns to explain events and emotions,

6. provide a conclusion,

7. organize the events so that they unfold naturally in the story.

Name_____ Date_____

Passage 11: Biography
Caroline Herschel: Astronomer

by Sarah B. Boyle

1   Lifting herself from housemaid to famous astronomer, Caroline Herschel wasn't your average eighteenth-century woman. By the time of her death, she had discovered a comet and become the first woman to be paid for her scientific studies.

2   Caroline Herschel was born on March 16, 1750, in Hanover, Germany, into a musical family. Isaak Herschel, Caroline's father, gave his children frequent music lessons when he was home from his job as a military musician. Both Caroline and her favorite brother, William, showed promise. But Caroline's mother, Anna Ilse Mortizen, insisted Caroline learn how to run a household. Though Caroline's father continued to give her music lessons in secret, Caroline spent most of her time doing housework. She was responsible for knitting all the socks for the family of twelve. She called herself the "Cinderella of the family."

3   Meanwhile, William had moved to England to teach music. In 1772, he returned to Hanover and invited Caroline to move to England with him. She agreed and left Germany to run his household there. She also assisted him in his musical career, singing along as he played the organ.

4   The Herschel family also loved the sciences. William, in particular, loved astronomy, or the study of heavenly bodies such as stars, planets, and comets. In the years that followed Caroline's coming to England, William's love of astronomy bloomed. Caroline joined him in his astronomy studies, just as she had in his music.

continued

Name_____ Date_____

5   Caroline's career as an astronomer began with assisting her brother. As William stood high on a ladder, peering through his telescope, he told Caroline what he saw. Caroline stood at his feet and recorded everything he said. Together, they documented 2,500 star clusters and other heavenly objects.

6   Soon, Caroline began studying and documenting the heavens on her own. She discovered fourteen nebulae, or large clusters of gas or dust in space. In 1786, Caroline watched as a distant object slowly traveled across the sky. Thrilled, she realized she had discovered a brand new comet. She wrote letters about her discovery to the astronomers she knew. And so she became the first woman to discover a comet.

7   Thanks to Caroline's discovery of the comet, King George III of England appointed her an official astronomer's assistant. And she became the first woman to receive payment for her scientific work. She was also the first woman to receive an honorary membership in the Royal Society of England, an organization of famous and influential scientists.

8   After William died in 1822, Caroline moved back to Germany. She died in Hanover at the age of 97, on January 9, 1841.

Name_____ Date_____

Close Reading 1: Read for Main Ideas and Details

"Caroline Herschel: Astronomer" is mostly about the first woman to discover a comet. Read the biography and underline the key details about Caroline Herschel's life. Then complete the graphic organizer using details from the biography. You can add to the graphic organizer if necessary.

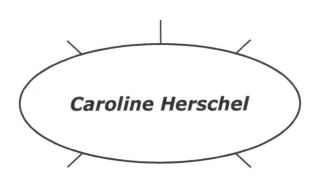

Collaborative Conversations

Discuss your answers with a partner. When you are the speaker, state your ideas and explain why you think each detail is important. When you are the listener, ask questions to clarify what the speaker says.

Sentence Frames

Speaker: A key detail about Caroline Herschel's life is . . .

I think the author included this detail so that . . .

Listener: Why did you choose this detail?

Could you tell me more about this idea?

Name_____ Date_____

Close Reading 2: Build Vocabulary

Reread the text. Locate each word or phrase, and identify context clues to determine its meaning. Underline the context clues as you read. Share your definitions or meanings with your partner and check your definitions using a dictionary.

Word or Phrase	Context Clues	What the Text Says It Means
responsible		
astronomy		
nebulae		
thrilled		
discovery		
honorary		

Think-Share-Write

Collaborate with your partner to generate new sentences showing your understanding of each word or phrase. Choose two of the new sentences and write them in the space below.

_____

_____

_____

_____

_____

Name_____ Date_____

Close Reading 3: Identify Text Structure Examples

Part I: Read and Annotate

In this text, the author mainly uses a sequence text structure to tell about Caroline Herschel's life. Reread the text and underline examples of this text structure. Be sure to underline any signal words or phrases used by the author that reinforce the author's use of the sequence text structure.

Part II: Collaborative Conversations

With a partner, discuss your examples using the following questions.

Discussion Questions	Our Notes
1. What text signal words helped you identify your examples?	
2. Did the author always use signal words? Explain how you were able to identify a relationship that did not include signal words.	
3. How does a sequence text structure help you understand the events that led to Caroline's discovery?	
4. Reread paragraph 1. The author begins Caroline Herschel's biography by summarizing her greatest accomplishments even though the text structure is sequence. How does this out-of-order information help you understand the text?	

Part III: Summarize

Write a quick summary of what the author tells you in paragraphs 2 and 3. Share your summary with a partner. How are your summaries similar? How are they different?

_____

_____

_____

Passage 11 • Biography

Name_____ Date_____

Close Reading 4: Build Deeper Understanding

Collaborative Conversations

Reread the text with a partner and discuss the questions. Use information from the text and your annotations to answer the questions. In your discussion, remember to express your ideas clearly and ask questions to better understand each other.

Close Reading Questions	Why did the author include the information about Caroline's childhood?	Was Caroline's discovery important? Why? How do you know?	Would Caroline have taken up astronomy if her brother hadn't been interested in it? Why or why not?
Text Evidence			
Inference/ Answer			

Name_____ Date_____

Apply Knowledge Through Writing

Part I: Collaborative Conversations

With a partner, read and analyze the prompt. Use the following questions in your discussion.

Writing Prompt

Imagine that you are Caroline Herschel, exploring the stars at a time when women were usually found in front of a stove instead of a telescope. Write a short story that describes how you found the new comet. Include descriptions of your thoughts and reactions, as well as the reactions of others. Use a sequence text structure for your story.

Analyze the Prompt	My Thoughts
Is this prompt informative/ explanatory or narrative?	
What is it asking me to write about?	
What are my ideas about this prompt?	

Part II: Write

Develop and write a short narrative. Be sure to . . .

1. begin the narrative by establishing a situation, including time and place,

2. introduce your characters or the narrator of the story,

3. use dialogue and description to develop characters and events,

4. use signal words to manage the sequence of events,

5. use strong verbs and nouns to explain events and emotions,

6. provide a conclusion,

7. organize the events so that they unfold naturally in the story.

Name_____ Date_____

Passage 12: Arts Article
Leonard Bernstein's Debut

from America's Library

1   Many people's careers begin after they get
a "break." On November 14, 1943, Leonard
Bernstein made his debut as a conductor for the
New York Philharmonic at Carnegie Hall in New
York City. This was Bernstein's "big break," and
a major turning point in his career. He got this
break because he was substituting for another
conductor, Bruno Walter, who had fallen ill.

2   Bernstein had been appointed assistant
conductor for the New York Philharmonic only a
few months before that night. Just twenty-five
years old, he was relatively inexperienced. At
the last minute, Bernstein was told he was to
take Walter's place, so he did not have any time
to rehearse. The music he was going to conduct
was very difficult. Plus, the concert was going to
be broadcast nationally on the radio. Despite all
these pressures, Bernstein rose to the occasion
and received a standing ovation at the end of the
concert. The event made national headlines, and
Bernstein became famous overnight.

Name_____ Date_____

3   Some people feel they do their best under the most stressful of circumstances. Have you ever been asked to do something you weren't prepared to do? How well were you able to perform? What was it about Leonard Bernstein that made him do so well in such a difficult situation?

4   Perhaps Leonard Bernstein did so well because music was his passion. The son of a man who supplied hairdressing products, Bernstein became interested in music at the age of ten. By the time he was a teenager, he was performing in public. He became a soloist with the Boston Public School Orchestra, and for thirteen weeks in 1934, he played classics on the radio.

Name_____ Date_____

Close Reading 1: Read for Main Ideas and Details

"Leonard Bernstein's Debut" is mostly about the first time Leonard Bernstein conducted the New York Philharmonic. Read the arts article and underline the details that explain the circumstances of his debut, or first performance. Then complete the graphic organizer using details from the arts article that discuss what happened after Bernstein's debut. You can add to the graphic organizer if necessary.

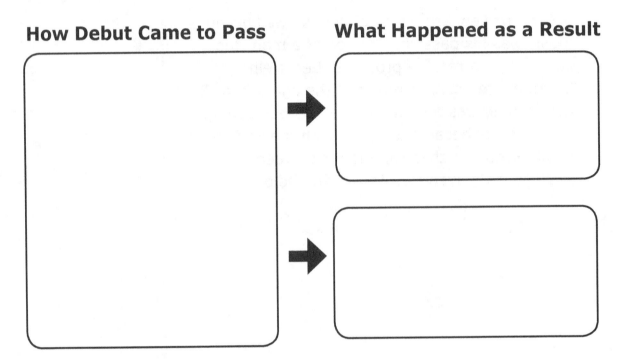

How Debut Came to Pass

What Happened as a Result

Collaborative Conversations

Discuss your answers with a partner. When you are the speaker, state the details you underlined and explain why you think they made Bernstein's task so difficult. When you are the listener, ask questions to clarify what the speaker says.

Sentence Frames

Speaker: One difficulty Bernstein faced was . . .

Based on the information in the text, this detail . . .

Listener: Why did you choose this detail?

Could you tell me more about this idea?

Name_____ Date_____

Close Reading 2: Build Vocabulary

Reread the text. Locate each word or phrase, and identify context clues to determine its meaning. Underline the context clues as you read. Share your definitions or meanings with your partner and check your definitions using a dictionary.

Word or Phrase	Context Clues	What the Text Says It Means
big break		
substituting		
rehearse		
broadcast		
pressures		

Think-Share-Write

Collaborate with your partner to generate new sentences showing your understanding of each word or phrase. Choose two of the new sentences and write them in the space below.

_____

_____

_____

_____

Name_____ Date_____

Close Reading 3: Identify Text Structure Examples

Part I: Read and Annotate

In this text, the author mainly uses a cause/effect text structure to share the story of Leonard Bernstein's debut. Reread the text and underline examples of this text structure. Be sure to underline any signal words or phrases used by the author that reinforce the author's use of the text structure.

Part II: Collaborative Conversations

With a partner, discuss your examples using the following questions.

Discussion Questions	Our Notes
1. What text signal words helped you identify your examples?	
2. Did the author always use signal words? Explain how you were able to identify a cause/effect relationship that did not include signal words.	
3. How does a cause/effect text structure help you understand the main idea of this text?	
4. Reread paragraph 4. The author tells about Bernstein's early life in chronological, or sequential, order. How does that help you understand the text?	

Part III: Summarize

Write a quick summary of what the author tells you in paragraphs 1 and 2. Share your summary with a partner. How are your summaries similar? How are they different?

_____

_____

_____

Name_____ Date_____

Close Reading 4: Build Deeper Understanding

Collaborative Conversations

Reread the text with a partner and discuss the questions. Use information from the text and your annotations to answer the questions. In your discussion, remember to express your ideas clearly and ask questions to better understand each other.

Close Reading Questions	Was Leonard Bernstein a famous conductor before November 14, 1943? How do you know?	Why did the author include information about Bernstein's childhood?	Would Bernstein have been as big of a success if Bruno Walter hadn't gotten sick that night?
Text Evidence			
Inference/ Answer			

Name_____ Date_____

Apply Knowledge Through Writing

Part I: Collaborative Conversations

With a partner, read and analyze the prompt. Use the following questions in your discussion.

Writing Prompt

It seems as if many people in the public eye become successful overnight. In reality, they have worked a long time to get where they are. Pick someone from your life who has a successful career or hobby. Write a short essay about how they came to be so good at what they do. Remember to support your ideas with detailed facts.

Analyze the Prompt	My Thoughts
Is this prompt informative/ explanatory or narrative?	
What is it asking me to write about?	
What are my ideas about this prompt?	

Part II: Write

Develop and write a short informative essay. Be sure to . . .

1. state your topic,

2. develop the topic using text evidence,

3. link ideas using appropriate words and phrases,

4. use vocabulary words related to the topic,

5. provide a conclusion,

6. organize your ideas in a meaningful way that aids comprehension.

Name_____ Date_____

Passage 13: Speech
excerpt from *We Shall Overcome*

by Lyndon B. Johnson

1 *President Lyndon B. Johnson delivered this speech (excerpted here) to the full U.S. Congress on Monday, March 15, 1965, to push for passage of the Voting Rights Act of 1965. President Johnson used the phrase "we shall overcome," borrowed from African American leaders struggling for equal rights. The term he used for African Americans—"Negroes"—was considered acceptable in the 1960s.*

2 As a man whose roots go deeply into Southern soil, I know how agonizing racial feelings are. I know how difficult it is to reshape the attitudes and the structure of our society. But a century has passed—more than 100 years—since the Negro was freed. And he is not fully free tonight. It was more than 100 years ago that Abraham Lincoln—a great President of another party— signed the Emancipation Proclamation. But emancipation is a proclamation and not a fact.

3 A century has passed—more than 100 years— since equality was promised, and yet the Negro is not equal. A century has passed since the day of promise, and the promise is unkept. The time of justice has now come, and I tell you that I believe sincerely that no force can hold it back. It is right in the eyes of man and God that it should come, and when it does, I think that day will brighten the lives of every American. For Negroes are not the only victims. How many white children have gone uneducated? How many white families have lived in stark poverty? How many white lives have been scarred by fear, because we wasted energy and our substance to maintain the barriers of hatred and terror?

continued

Name_____ Date_____

4   And so I say to all of you here and to all in the nation tonight that those who appeal to you to hold on to the past do so at the cost of denying you your future. This great rich, restless country can offer opportunity and education and hope to all—all, black and white, North and South, sharecropper and city dweller. These are the enemies: poverty, ignorance, disease. They are our enemies, not our fellow man, not our neighbor.

5   And these enemies too—poverty, disease and ignorance—we shall overcome.

Name_____ Date_____

Close Reading 1: Read for Main Ideas and Details

"We Shall Overcome" is mostly about the need for all people to have the same rights, no matter who they are or what they look like. Read the speech and underline the key details that support the text's main idea. Then complete the graphic organizer using details from the speech. You can add to the graphic organizer if necessary.

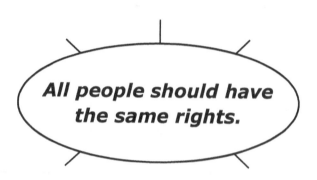

All people should have the same rights.

Collaborative Conversations

Discuss your answers with a partner. When you are the speaker, state the details you underlined and explain why you think they support the main idea of the text. When you are the listener, ask questions to clarify what the speaker says.

Sentence Frames

Speaker: The author explores the idea that . . .

A key detail that supports this idea is . . .

Listener: Why did you choose this detail?

What evidence in the text leads you to say that?

Name_____ Date_____

Close Reading 2: Build Vocabulary

Reread the text. Locate each word or phrase, and identify context clues to determine its meaning. Underline the context clues as you read. Share your definitions or meanings with your partner and check your definitions using a dictionary.

Word or Phrase	Context Clues	What the Text Says It Means
attitudes		
century		
unkept		
appeal		
denying		
enemies		

Think-Share-Write

Collaborate with your partner to generate new sentences showing your understanding of each word or phrase. Choose two of the new sentences and write them in the space below.

_____

_____

_____

_____

Name_____ Date_____

Close Reading 3: Identify Text Structure Examples

Part I: Read and Annotate

In this text, the author mainly uses compare/contrast text structure to explain the need for all people to be treated equally. Reread the text and underline examples of this text structure. Be sure to underline any signal words or phrases used by the author that reinforce the author's use of the compare/contrast text structure.

Part II: Collaborative Conversations

With a partner, discuss your examples using the following questions.

Discussion Questions	Our Notes
1. What text signal words helped you identify your examples?	
2. Did the author always use signal words? Explain how you were able to identify a relationship that did not include signal words.	
3. How does a compare/contrast text structure help you understand the main idea of this text?	
4. The president also uses descriptive language to explain his position. Identify some examples from paragraphs 3 and 4. How does the use of this language make you feel? What does it make you think about? How does it impact your understanding of Johnson's main point?	

Part III: Summarize

Write a quick summary of what the author tells you in paragraphs 2 and 3. Share your summary with a partner. How are your summaries similar? How are they different?

_____

_____

Name_____ Date_____

Close Reading 4: Build Deeper Understanding

Collaborative Conversations

Reread the text with a partner and discuss the questions. Use information from the text and your annotations to answer the questions. In your discussion, remember to express your ideas clearly and ask questions to better understand each other.

Close Reading Questions	Who is the audience for this speech?	Why did the president say that African Americans weren't fully freed?	Why did the president use the phrase "we shall overcome" in his speech?
Text Evidence			
Inference/ Answer			

Name_____ Date_____

Apply Knowledge Through Writing

Part I: Collaborative Conversations

With a partner, read and analyze the prompt. Use the following questions in your discussion.

Writing Prompt

Public figures make speeches to share their opinions with the public and to convince the public that a certain viewpoint is correct. Imagine that you are a political leader, like a mayor, governor, or even president. Write a speech about a topic that you feel strongly about, such as global warming, education, animal rights, or hunger. Remember to include facts and ideas that support your main idea.

Analyze the Prompt	My Thoughts
Is this prompt informative/ explanatory or opinion/argument?	
What is it asking me to write about?	
What are my ideas about this prompt?	

Part II: Write

Develop and write a short opinion essay. Be sure to . . .

1. introduce the topic,

2. state your opinion,

3. support your opinion with reasons based on text evidence,

4. use linking words and phrases that connect your opinion and reasons,

5. provide a conclusion,

6. organize your ideas in a meaningful way to support your opinion.

Name_____ Date_____

Passage 14: Biography
Help for the Hard Times

from America's Library

1   George Washington Carver was born a slave in Diamond Grove, Missouri, around 1864. He became one of the nation's most famous agricultural scientists. He is best known for his research on peanuts. He wanted to help poor African American farmers.

2   Carver wanted to share his knowledge and research with other African Americans. He was especially committed to helping poor black farmers. He had lots of advice on how to become more "thrifty and self-supporting." So when he was working at Tuskegee Institute, he wrote many educational booklets for farmers. One booklet was "Help for the Hard Times."

3   First, Carver said farmers should plant a garden. He said that a "good garden" can provide half of the family food. When Carver was writing, many poor farmers grew only one crop, cotton, for money. While many of those farmers knew a lot about growing cotton, they didn't know much about growing vegetables or herbs. In "Help for the Hard Times," Carver used simple language to explain how to start a garden, when to plant, and what to plant.

4   There's no need to buy chemical fertilizers to get the soil ready. Carver said to use what nature provides: leaves, soil from the woods and "muck from the rich swamps." He said to plant potatoes, peas, and spinach, as well as other vegetables and herbs, in February, and to plant cauliflower, collards, and watermelon in March.

Name_____ Date_____

5   By April, most of the garden should be growing and only a few things like cabbage, eggplant and cotton seed need to be planted. Carver also had lots of suggestions for making money.

6   Carver believed in feeding the family, selling the extras, and using the money to buy more resources like animals or seeds. His first suggestion for making money was to have "12 good hens and 1 rooster." The chickens would lay enough eggs to feed the family and there would be extras to sell. If some of the eggs hatched, the new chickens could also be sold.

7   Carver also believed in making things instead of buying them. In "Help for the Hard Times" he suggested making things to sell: wood shingles, fence posts, baskets, quilts, and lace. He also suggested making and selling fruit and vegetable preserves.

8   Farmers could earn good money with a few hogs. Carver said to buy young hogs. Hogs are cheap to raise because they eat leftover slop, rotten vegetables, and weeds. Once they're big enough, they can be turned into sausage, meat, and lard, which are guaranteed to sell. If a family can afford it, they should also buy a cow, which Carver said would provide "at least half the family's living."

9   For Carver, there was no waste in nature. Everything could be put to use. Carver believed that even the poorest farmers could improve their standard of living if they put to use all that nature had to offer.

Name_____ Date_____

Close Reading 1: Read for Main Ideas and Details

Passage 14 • Biography

"Help for the Hard Times" is mostly about the information George Washington Carver wanted to share with the African American community. Read the biography and underline the details Carver shared to help his readers. Then complete the graphic organizer using details from the article. You can add to the graphic organizer if necessary.

Things to Grow	Things to Make	Things to Sell

Collaborative Conversations

Discuss your answers with a partner. When you are the speaker, state your ideas and explain why you think each detail supports Carver's thoughts about getting through the hard times. When you are the listener, ask questions to clarify what the speaker says.

Sentence Frames

Speaker: The author explores the idea that . . .

A key idea that supports Carver's main idea is . . .

Listener: Why did you choose this detail?

Could you tell me more about this idea?

Name_____ Date_____

Close Reading 2: Build Vocabulary

Locate each word or phrase, and identify context clues to determine its meaning. Underline the context clues as you read. Share your definitions or meanings with your partner and check your definitions using a dictionary.

Word or Phrase	Context Clues	What the Text Says It Means
herbs		
chemical fertilizers		
nature		
resources		
preserves		
living		

Think-Share-Write

Collaborate with your partner to generate new sentences showing your understanding of each word or phrase. Choose two of the new sentences and write them in the space below.

_____

_____

_____

_____

Name_____ Date_____

Close Reading 3: Identify Text Structure Examples

Part I: Read and Annotate

In this text, the author mainly uses descriptive text structure to tell about the information Carver shared in his book. Reread the text and underline examples of this text structure. Be sure to underline any signal words or phrases used by the author that reinforce the author's use of the descriptive text structure.

Part II: Collaborative Conversations

With a partner, discuss your examples using the following questions.

Discussion Questions	Our Notes
1. What text signal words helped you identify your examples?	
2. Did the author always use signal words? Explain how you were able to identify a relationship that did not include signal words.	
3. How does a descriptive text structure help you understand the main idea of this text?	
4. Reread paragraph 1. The author introduces the text by presenting a problem, then uses the rest of the text to show the solution. How does this structure help you better understand the information presented in the text?	

Part III: Summarize

Write a quick summary of what the author tells you in paragraphs 3 and 4. Share your summary with a partner. How are your summaries similar? How are they different?

_____

_____

Name_____ Date_____

Close Reading 4: Build Deeper Understanding

Collaborative Conversations

Reread the text with a partner and discuss the questions. Use information from the text and your annotations to answer the questions. In your discussion, remember to express your ideas clearly and ask questions to better understand each other.

Close Reading Questions	Why did George Washington Carver name his booklet "Help for the Hard Times"?	Why did Carver feel that he had to teach farmers how to grow food?	What might Carver say to farmers who said they couldn't plant their own vegetables because they had too much work already?
Text Evidence			
Inference/ Answer			

Name_____ Date_____

Apply Knowledge Through Writing

Part I: Collaborative Conversations

With a partner, read and analyze the prompt. Use the following questions in your discussion.

Writing Prompt

Even though it was written more than 100 years ago, some of the information shared in "Help for the Hard Times" is still useful today. Think about advice you would give to someone who has fallen on hard times. Write a short essay describing how a person can improve his or her living situation by using things in nature or by using things they already have.

Analyze the Prompt	My Thoughts
Is this prompt informative/ explanatory or narrative?	
What is it asking me to write about?	
What are my ideas about this prompt?	

Part II: Write

Develop and write a short informative essay. Be sure to . . .

1. state your topic,

2. develop the topic using text evidence,

3. link ideas using appropriate words and phrases,

4. use vocabulary words related to the topic,

5. provide a conclusion,

6. organize your ideas in a meaningful way that aids comprehension.

Sentence Frames

Speaker: A key idea that supports the main idea is . . . .

I know this because . . . .

Listener: Why did you choose this detail?

What evidence in the text leads you to say that?

Speaker: The main characters are . . . .

The main problem in the story is . . . .

Listener: What details does the author use to describe this?

What can you tell from that?

Speaker: This detail is important because . . . .

Based on the information in the text . . . .

Listener: Could you tell me more about that detail?

What details does the author use to describe that?

Speaker: The speaker's main point is . . . .

Based on the information in the speech. . . .

Listener: What information in the speech leads you to say that?

What details does the speaker use to describe that?

Speaker: This detail makes me think . . . .

The author explores the idea that . . . .

Listener: Why did you choose that detail?

Why did the author include this detail?

Rubrics

Narrative Writing Checklist

	Yes	No	Not Sure
1. My narrative has a strong lead that catches the reader's attention.			
2. I include specific details to establish the time, place, and characters involved.			
3. I use dialogue to develop experiences and events and to show the responses of characters to situations			
4. I include description to help my readers visualize the events and characters.			
5. I include dialogue or express what people said.			
6. My narrative is logically sequenced.			
7. I use sequence (transitional) words and phrases to manage the sequence of events.			
8. My narrative has a strong ending.			
9. I tell my personal narrative using kid-friendly language.			
10. I use describing words, including adjectives and adverbs, to tell my story.			
11. I use both concrete and sensory language, to convey experiences and events precisely.			
12. I provide a conclusion that follows from the experiences and events in my narrative.			

Quality Writing Checklist

I looked for and corrected ...	Yes	No	Not Sure
sentence fragments and run-ons.			
parts of speech (pronouns, auxiliaries, adjectives, prepositions).			
grammar.			
indented paragraphs.			
punctuation.			
capitalization.			
spelling.			

Writing Checklists

Rubrics

Informative/Explanatory Writing Checklist

	Yes	No	Not Sure
1. I researched my topic and organized my information into notes that helped me write my text.			
2. I introduce my topic clearly and use words that grab my readers' attention.			
3. I keep my paper organized by grouping information together in a way that makes sense. I use paragraphs and sections.			
4. I use headings to organize my sections.			
5. The information in my report is accurate.			
6. I support my points with facts, definitions, concrete details, and quotations.			
7. I include graphics to support my information.			
8. I include captions that explain each graphic.			
9. I use linking words and phrases to connect ideas.			
10. My report includes different viewpoints so that I do not sway my readers to think one way.			
11. I include a strong conclusion that keeps my readers thinking.			
12. I choose words that make my text interesting to read and easy to understand. I include words that connect to the topic.			
13. I use at least one primary source.			
14. I use a formal voice.			

Quality Writing Checklist

I looked for and corrected . . .	Yes	No	Not Sure
sentence fragments and run-ons.			
parts of speech (pronouns, auxiliaries, adjectives, prepositions).			
grammar.			
indented paragraphs.			
punctuation.			
capitalization.			
spelling.			

Rubrics

Opinion/Argument Writing Checklist

	Yes	No	Not Sure
1. I introduce my topic with a lead that grabs my readers' attention.			
2. I state my opinion at the beginning of my paper.			
3. I include reasons for my opinion based on my own thoughts about the topic.			
4. I group connected ideas together.			
5. I use evidence from the text to support my opinion.			
6. I use linking words, signal words, and phrases to link ideas.			
7. I include a concluding sentence or paragraph that makes my readers think.			
8. My opinion follows an organized structure.			
9. I choose words that make sense and make my opinion interesting.			
10. I do not change my opinion.			
11. I use different types of sentences.			
12. I use my voice to show people how much I care about my opinion.			

Quality Writing Checklist

I looked for and corrected . . .	Yes	No	Not Sure
sentence fragments and run-ons.			
parts of speech (pronouns, auxiliaries, adjectives, prepositions).			
grammar.			
indented paragraphs.			
punctuation.			
capitalization.			
spelling.			

Writing Checklists

Notes:

Notes: